D1564614

ACHIEVING EQUITABLE ACCESS

A*CHIEVING* E*QUITABLE* A*CCESS*

STUDIES OF HEALTH CARE ISSUES AFFECTING

HISPANICS AND AFRICAN AMERICANS

MARSHA D. LILLIE-BLANTON

WILHELMINA A. LEIGH

ANA I. ALFARO-CORREA

editors

Joint Center for Political and Economic Studies

The Joint Center for Political and Economic Studies is a national, nonprofit institution that conducts research on public policy issues of special concern to black Americans and promotes informed and effective involvement of blacks in the governmental process. Founded in 1970, the Joint Center provides independent and nonpartisan analyses through research, publication, and outreach programs.

Opinions expressed in Joint Center publications are those of the authors and do not necessarily reflect the views of the staff, officers, or governors of the Joint Center or of the organizations supporting the Center and its research.

Distributed by arrangement with University Press of America
4720 Boston Way
Lanham, MD 20706

3 Henrietta Street
London WC2E 8LU England

Library of Congress Cataloging-in-Publication Data
Achieving equitable access: studies of health care issues affecting Hispanics
    and African-Americans / edited by Marsha Lillie-Blanton, Wilhelmina
    Leigh, and Ana Alfaro-Correa.
    p.   cm.
    Includes bibliographical references and index.
    1. Afro-Americans—Medical care. 2. Hispanic Americans—Medical care.
3. Health services accessibility—United States.   4. Medical care—Utiliza-
tion—United States. I. Lillie-Blanton, Marsha. II. Leigh, Wilhelmina. III.
Alfaro-Correa, Ana.
RA448.4.B37   1996   362.1'089'68073-dc20   96-20122   CIP
ISBN 0-7618-0377-7 (cloth: alk. paper)
ISBN 0-7618-0378-5 (pbk.: alk. paper)

The Joint Center gratefully acknowledges the support of The Commonwealth Fund and the Ford Foundation in making this publication possible. We also wish to thank the Rockefeller and Prudential Foundations for support of our health policy research program, as well as numerous general support donors for their continuing generosity.

Foreword

In the past thirty years, the United States has made remarkable progress in reducing barriers to health care faced by racial and ethnic minority Americans. Most minority Americans born before 1950 have vivid memories of separate and unequal health facilities. By the 1980s, however, blatant barriers to care had become uncommon, and improved access to medical care existed for significant numbers of Americans. Yet in spite of this progress, African Americans and Hispanics—the two largest racial/ethnic minorities—continue to endure unequal access to health care compared to non-Hispanic whites.

These remaining disparities will have to be addressed in the context of a changing health-care system. While the comprehensive reform promised in the 1993 Clinton health plan is not likely to be realized, numerous other proposals have been made to modify Medicaid and Medicare and to tinker at the margins of the public/private health care system. They have implications for all Americans, but particularly for those who are currently disadvantaged in terms of health care access. Developing policies that improve access for Hispanics and African Americans will require that we understand more about how and why these groups are disadvantaged compared to whites.

To investigate differences in access to health care, a three-year research and public policy initiative was undertaken by the Joint Center for Political and Economic Studies, with support from The Commonwealth Fund. The research component was led by a core group based at the Johns Hopkins University School of Public Health, while the Joint Center had primary responsibility for coordinating the project, including organizing policy forums and publicizing the results of the research.

The project's goal was to provide information to guide policymakers, practitioners, and advocates in making decisions about health-care issues of particular concern to Hispanics and African Americans. To achieve this goal, the project convened two public policy forums and analyzed relevant data sources. The Joint Center published the key public policy findings in a summary report, *In the Nation's*

Interest: Equity in Access to Health Care. With this volume we are making available the papers produced by each research team.

Teams composed of Hispanic, African American, and white researchers from across the country were commissioned to examine the health-care experiences of nonelderly Hispanics and African Americans using a nationally representative data source, the 1987 National Medical Expenditure Survey (NMES). The use of NMES data permitted a population-based assessment of access to health care. Researchers were challenged to identify key issues for which new knowledge could assist in shaping policy goals and redirecting the behavior of health care providers and of individuals seeking improved access to care. In their studies, the authors document the extent to which differences in access persist and provide insight concerning the causes of these differences. In addition to offering new perspectives on health-care access, the project provides the most comprehensive analysis of the NMES data ever undertaken on Hispanics and African Americans.

The project was conducted under the supervision of Dr. Milton D. Morris, vice president for research at the Joint Center. Dr. Marsha D. Lillie-Blanton, assistant professor of health policy and management at the Johns Hopkins University School of Public Health, directed the Johns Hopkins research effort, and Dr. Wilhelmina A. Leigh, senior research associate, coordinated the project at the Joint Center. These two scholars, along with Dr. Ana I. Alfaro-Correa, research fellow in epidemiology and preventive medicine at the University of Maryland School of Medicine, edited this volume. We salute their efforts. We also acknowledge the contributions made by participants in the policy forums and by other researchers, including Dr. Antonio Furino, Dr. Alvin Headen, Dr. LaRah Payne, and Dr. Rueben Warren, who reviewed earlier drafts of the papers. A sincere thanks goes to Dr. Karen Scott Collins, assistant vice president of The Commonwealth Fund, for her helpful suggestions throughout the project.

Of course, a special thanks is extended to The Commonwealth Fund and its president, Dr. Karen Davis, without whom none of this would have been possible.

Eddie N. Williams
President, Joint Center for Political and Economic Studies

Contents

List of Tables and Figures

Tables

Figures

Introduction

Americans enjoy the best health care in the world, it is often said. But while many Americans have access to the finest care and up-to-date technology, others, including many members of racial and ethnic minority groups, have a much different experience with the health-care system, often receiving inferior or inadequate care or even no care at all. In the past thirty years, the United States has made remarkable progress in reducing barriers in access to health care faced by racial and ethnic minority Americans; nevertheless, recent studies show that these populations continue to experience unequal degrees of access to health coverage and treatment procedures. Knowledge of the scope, nature, and causes of these lingering differentials in access, however, has been limited.

This book is the culmination of a project to advance knowledge about the remaining barriers experienced by Hispanics and African Americans seeking health-care services. These two population groups are quite different, yet they share a commonality of experiences. Both Hispanics and African Americans have faced a history of discriminatory policies and practices that have reduced their access to care as well as their access to training opportunities in the health professions. Both population groups have cultural beliefs and practices that sometimes conflict with Western medicine. As such, some impediments to care may be self-imposed, the result of personal preferences and a lack of confidence in the medical system. Also, both population groups are likely to live in segregated neighborhoods and experience poverty rates three times that of whites. Moreover, many Hispanic and African American neighborhoods are less attractive practice sites to health-care providers and, thus, are medically underserved. By focusing on these two groups, the hope is to forge greater understanding of problem areas and policy options that are common to both, while also identifying those that are population-specific.

Using a nationally representative data source, the 1987 National Medical Expenditure Survey, the research teams examined a number of widely used access indicators to gauge where this nation currently stands in reducing barriers to care. Access to care was defined broadly to include both the potential to obtain services (e.g., insurance coverage and regular sources of care) and actual use of services (e.g., physician visits and health-care expenditures). Researchers used various analytic techniques to understand the extent to which factors such as ethnic subgroup, financial burden, usual source of care, language, attitudes, and beliefs influence racial/ethnic variations in access. The teams used a common data source and set of key definitions; however, the studies differed in the specific population subgroups examined and in the access indicators investigated. The project attempted to achieve some uniformity of purpose while allowing investigators an opportunity to pursue their independent ideas and interests. This book, the project's final product, presents the papers produced by the research teams.

The commissioned studies are presented in two sections. Part I is composed of four chapters that investigate financial and sociocultural barriers to care, while Part II focuses on how to improve timely, appropriate use of health services.

Since financial and sociocultural barriers influence the behavior of the population in need of care and the providers of care, the chapters in Part I describe the characteristics of both types of barriers and examine how relationships between them affect who gets care and where care is obtained. The first chapter compares the characteristics of Hispanics and African Americans who seek care from physicians of their own racial/ethnic group with the characteristics of those who obtain care from physicians of other racial/ethnic groups. Chapter 2 looks at the socioeconomic and health determinants of three indicators of the use of health services: the likelihood of having a blood pressure check, the likelihood of an ambulatory care visit, and the average number of ambulatory visits. Health services use is examined for whites, African Americans, and Mexican Americans. Chapter 3 assesses differences in the financial burden of health care for whites, Hispanics, and African Americans, using several measures of health expenditures, including total expenditures, out-of-pocket costs, and premiums. The final chapter in this section explores determinants of a usual source of care among Puerto Ricans, Mexican Americans, and a combined group of all other Hispanic subpopulations.

The chapters in Part II focus on two areas of concern: first, the use of services when the need for care may be critical (e.g. for chronic conditions such as hypertension) or at more costly sites (e.g., hospital-based sources of care); second, the impacts of potential changes in federal and state roles in health care on services received by uninsured or underinsured persons. The first chapter in this section (Chapter 5) examines factors linked to the frequent use of hospital-based outpatient services by Hispanics and African Americans. To identify the factors most strongly associated with the use of hospital outpatient departments (OPDs), the characteristics of persons who report that their regular source of care is a hospital OPD are compared to the characteristics of those who regularly see a private physician in his or her office. Barriers to care among hypertensives are the subject of Chapter 6, which examines the extent to which differences in factors such as insurance coverage, having a usual source of care, distance to provider, and fluency in English posed barriers to care for a population known to have greater than average medical care needs. In Chapter 7, the authors examine whether cultural or attitudinal factors might explain the use by whites, Hispanics, and African Americans of hospital emergency rooms for non-urgent conditions. The final chapter in this section identifies constitutional and statutory provisions that guide federal/ state roles in health care and examines the effect of these provisions on access to care by minority populations within and across geographic regions of the United States.

At the end of the book is a summary of the researchers' key findings and suggestions for public policy initiatives to achieve further gains in access. This section was adapted from the project's summary report, *In the Nation's Interest: Equity in Access to Health Care* (published by the Joint Center for Political and Economic Studies in 1995) with the intent of linking the research findings with a general discussion of their policy implications.

SETTING FUTURE DIRECTIONS

This assessment of access to health care occurs at a critical period in the nation's history. The national system for financing and delivering health care that has evolved since the 1960s has been the subject of considerable debate. While the debate has shifted away from

3

discussions of comprehensive national health reforms, pressures to control health-care costs are slowly transforming the systems of health financing and delivery. Particular emphasis is being placed on the restructuring of public-sector health programs, with associated implications for private facilities and programs. Established primarily to improve access for poor and medically underserved populations, public-sector programs such as Medicaid and Medicare greatly benefit minority group Americans who are disproportionately poor.

As efforts to restructure these programs are underway, this book serves as an information source on the nation's progress in expanding access through some of these public initiatives. Its important, timely contributions to a solid knowledge base on the racial/ethnic inequalities in access to health care will help in setting a research agenda and policy goals for the future. Individually, each chapter addresses a different subject; together, they provide an update on the progress achieved and the challenges that remain in creating a health-care system that can equitably serve all Americans, regardless of race or ethnicity.

PART I

Reducing Financial and Sociocultural Barriers to Care

CHAPTER 1

The Effect of Ethnic/Racial Matches Between Provider and Patient on the Use of Health Services by Hispanics and African Americans

Felipe G. Castro, Kathryn Coe, and Mary Harmon

According to a number of sources, members of the two largest
ethnic/racial minority populations in the United States, African
Americans and Hispanics, experience higher rates of morbidity and
mortality and face greater barriers in access to medical care, compared with members of the non-Hispanic white population (de la
Cancela 1992; Hale 1992; Harper and Lambert 1994). Both socioeconomic and psychological barriers seem to prevent African Americans
and Hispanics from entering the health-care system or to inhibit
them from establishing a regular source of health care. These
barriers include fear of the diagnosis of a fatal illness, concerns
about the loss of wages, cultural beliefs and values related to the
treatment and prevention of disease, lack of money and health
insurance coverage, transportation problems, and long waiting times.
Moreover, for some Hispanics, language may also operate as a
barrier to health care.

An additional barrier for African American and Hispanic patients, not
only in the initial search for health services but also in their continu-
ation and compliance with treatment, is a health provider with low
cultural competence; that is, one who lacks an understanding of and
sensitivity to cultural differences and patient needs associated with
these differences. Cultural competence is defined as an active
understanding of a person's culture, social norms, mores, and
sanctions, as these influence behavior and reactions to illness
(Orlandi 1992). A physician will probably have the greatest cultural
competence in dealing with those persons of his own culture. When

a patient sees a physician from his or her own ethnic/racial group, this cultural similarity between patient and physician is likely to facilitate more effective patient-physician communications and social bonding.

Within this matching perspective, it is also recognized that simply having a physician from the patient's own ethnic/racial background will not necessarily guarantee physician sensitivity and competence in addressing the patient's medical needs. Nonetheless, on average, greater congruence in patient-physician cultural backgrounds and experiences, as depicted by physician-patient cultural matches, would be expected to promote better treatment and better health outcomes relative to physician-patient nonmatches. Based on this perspective, patient-physician match is the focus of the present study.

OVERVIEW OF PRIOR RESEARCH

According to recent studies, African Americans and Hispanics have disproportionately high rates of morbidity and mortality for the major chronic degenerative diseases (Harper and Lambert 1994). Chronic degenerative diseases, AIDS, violence (leading to injury or death), cancer, cardiovascular disease, and diabetes mellitus account for a higher percentage of deaths among African Americans and Hispanics than among non-Hispanic whites (de la Cancela 1992; Haffner et al. 1991; Westbrook, Brown, and McBride 1975).

African Americans are the largest racial/ethnic group in the United States, with a population of nearly 33 million. The relatively poor health status of many African Americans, compared to non-Hispanic whites, is indicated by an age-adjusted risk of death nationally of 2:1 or greater for infant mortality, homicide, diabetes mellitus, and AIDS. When compared with rates for non-Hispanic whites, these disease-specific rates contribute to an overall age-adjusted relative risk for all causes of death of 6:1 for African Americans.

Hispanics are the second largest ethnic/racial population in the United States, with a population of 22.8 million as of March 1993. The Hispanic population of the United States consists of persons of any race who are members of one of five major Spanish-origin subgroups: Mexican Americans (14.63 million), Puerto Ricans (2.40 million), Cubans (1.07 million), Central and South Americans (3.05

million), and "other Hispanics" (1.60 million) (Montgomery 1994). This diverse Hispanic population contains large numbers of working poor whose jobs offer few or no health insurance benefits, thus limiting their access to health care (Ginzberg 1991). This lack of health insurance is regarded as one of the most serious barriers that Hispanics face in obtaining needed health services (Giachello 1994). Moreover, among Hispanics, and primarily among certain subgroups of Mexican Americans and Puerto Ricans, there are significant health problems reflected in high rates of diabetes mellitus, hypertension, tuberculosis, HIV infection, alcoholism, certain cancers, and violent death (Council on Scientific Affairs 1991).

Research on use of health-care services has documented that members of ethnic/racial minority groups, compared with the members of the mainstream society, are significantly less likely to initiate preventive care, are less likely to have a regular source of health care, and make fewer medical visits per year (Lewin-Epstein 1991). This pattern of underutilization holds for preventive and curative care for physical health ailments, as well as care for mental and dental problems (Flaskerud and Li-tze 1992).

Wells et al. (1987) have postulated that Hispanics may view seeking health care for mental disorders with greater stigma than do non-Hispanic whites and, consequently, avoid such care. Similarly, White and Parham (1990) indicate that in seeking mental health services, many African Americans are hesitant to entrust their life stories and pain to a non-black person. This guardedness is understandable, particularly in a client-therapist nonmatch in which the therapist or physician, who is from another ethnic/racial group, exhibits cultural insensitivity to family systems, to traditional support networks, and to norms, values, and expectations that prevail within the African American patient's local community.

Various studies have identified socioeconomic factors as major barriers that delay the entry of African Americans and Hispanics into the health-care system and prevent them from pursuing an ongoing medical regimen or inhibit them from receiving monitoring for their health. Thus, ethnic/racial minorities in the lower socioeconomic strata seek health services at lower rates than do members of the mainstream white population at the same strata (Leaf et al. 1987). Such underutilization is largely due to the high cost of health care and to lack of health insurance, resulting partly from unemployment (Quesada and Heller 1977). Further, these personal economic factors are closely linked to other factors that also act as barriers, such as governmental policies that limit access to health care and the unavailability of certain health services (Treviño et al. 1992; Walker 1992).

While the effects of structural and economic factors have dominated research on health-seeking behavior, other factors that may work independently or synergistically with structural and economic factors have received less attention. These other factors center around culture and include acculturation, language, use of traditional medicine, and psychological factors such as feelings of trust and confidence in the medical system, and, more specifically, trust and confidence in the physician or other direct-service provider. Central to the potential resolution of these cultural disparities is the cultural match between the patient and the health provider.

Harwood (1981) has proposed guidelines for clinicians and practitioners who wish to provide culturally appropriate health care to members of ethnic/racial groups. Assuming that the provider is not a member of the same ethnic/racial group as the patient, Harwood indicates that providers must determine, as part of their early interaction with patients, the unique personal history and cultural orientation of their patients. This patient assessment includes asking about prior experiences with health education, previous experiences with a given illness, urban or rural origin, and level of formal education. For immigrants, the assessment should also determine age at immigration to this country and the degree of encapsulation within an ethnic and family social network. In short, the provider must obtain certain information in order to understand the patient's sociocultural context.

Among Hispanics, level of acculturation and level of assimilation to mainstream social norms have been identified as significant moderators of health behavior (Dana 1993). A number of studies have observed that a lower level of acculturation is associated with a lower rate of health service utilization (Andersen, Lewis, and Giachello 1981; Elder et al. 1991). This pattern of lower utilization has been attributed to an unfamiliarity with services or a distrust of the medical system and has been observed in several areas of health care, but especially mental health care. For example, Wells and colleagues (1987) found that less-acculturated Hispanics with functional impairment due to physical or mental disorders exhibited significantly lower rates of mental health service use.

Among some monolingual Spanish-speaking Hispanics, access solely to a medical system without bilingual/bicultural staff is another barrier that may affect physician-patient rapport and compromise medical treatment. For less-acculturated Hispanics, primarily those who are only able to communicate in Spanish, lack of access to a bilingual/bicultural provider can impede the patient's search for treatment and compliance with medical regimens. However, even when patient and provider speak the same language, the cultural orientation of the patient and the cultural competence of the provider may influence the *effectiveness* of their communication and the establishment of rapport, which can ultimately influence the quality of health care (Roter, Hall, and Katz 1988). When a communication barrier exists between the client and the provider, whether this barrier is linguistic or interpersonal, the patient may feel misunderstood or mistreated. He may believe that the medical treatment received will be an inappropriate or unacceptable remedy for a given illness. Thus, since the type of language used may influence the patient's concepts and comprehension of health and illness, the physician should elicit the patient's concept of disease and should express information about the current disease/illness in terms that the patient understands (Gomez, Ruiz, and Rumbaut 1985). This will help to avoid miscommunication about diseases and symptoms.

In addition to issues of acculturation and language, the provision of culturally appropriate health care requires consideration of a number of other issues. First, as Harwood (1981) and others (Castro et al. 1992; de la Cancela 1992) have recognized, health providers must demonstrate proficiency in addressing Hispanics and members of other ethnic/racial groups in a way that respects their values, beliefs, attitudes, and behaviors. This approach explicitly avoids viewing Hispanics in stereotypical or in deficit-laden ways. For example, a health provider may believe that "machismo" is a typical Hispanic male trait and that it serves as a barrier to compliance with medical regimens. While this may be true for some Hispanic males, this belief and a provider's negative attitude toward macho males may prejudice the provider and interfere with his judgment about the treatment (de la Cancela 1992).

While providers must become culturally competent, they must also recognize the extensive within-group diversity found within the large African American and Hispanic populations and avoid viewing members of these populations in stereotypical ways that attribute a trait or characteristic to all members of this group. For example, within the major national Hispanic groups (Puerto Ricans, Cubans, and Mexican Americans), there are subgroups with considerable variation among their members. Given that individual members of ethnic groups are a product of their unique social and cultural history, it should not be assumed that their health beliefs and practices are shared with the mainstream society or necessarily with other members of their own ethnic group or subgroup (Castro, Furth, and Karlow 1984). It is important that the health provider examine the whole person and his or her own unique patterns of belief and behavior in the context that person's cultural, ethnic, and racial community (de la Cancela 1992).

METHODS

Data for Hispanics and African Americans were analyzed from the 1987 National Medical Expenditure Survey (NMES). A series of conditional statements were used to identify physician-patient matches and nonmatches by ethnic/racial status. In developing these matches, it was recognized that the Bureau of the Census asserts that persons of Hispanic origin can be of *any* race (Montgomery 1994). Thus, beyond their self-identified racial status, for Hispanic patients, self-identification as a member of any one of five major Hispanic groups was used to categorize them as Hispanics. Patients who self-identified as Mexican Americans, Puerto Ricans, Cubans, other Hispanics, or Spanish were thus categorized as *Hispanic patients.* Similarly, for medical providers, those who were identified as the usual doctors of these patients were considered for matching status. Physicians who self-identified according to one of the five major Hispanic categories were categorized as *Hispanic physicians.*

For African American patients, the term *African American* was recognized as referring to an identity that is cultural as well as racial (Pinderhughes 1982). Thus, in the present study, the patient's self-identification according to the racial/ethnic labels of black or African American was used to categorize patients as *African American patients*. Similarly, medical providers who were identified as usual doctors of these patients and who self-identified as black or African American were categorized as *African American physicians*.

Hispanic physician-patient matches were defined by selection criteria in which the patient was classified, as described above, as being Hispanic, and where the physician also was classified as being Hispanic. Hispanic nonmatches were those cases where the patient was classified as being Hispanic, but the physician was classified as being of another ethnic/racial background, including non-Hispanic White, African American, Asian/Pacific Islander, or Native American/ American Indian.

Similarly for African Americans, physician-patient matches were defined as those cases where both patient and physician self-reported their ethnic/racial identity as being African American. Conversely, African American nonmatches were defined as cases where the usual physician of African American patients was from a different ethnic/racial group.

This study first examined patient background characteristics by patient-physician matching status: (1) matches and (2) nonmatches. These analyses of patient background characteristics were conducted separately for African Americans and for Hispanics. The patient background variables examined in this study were: self-rating of health, marital status, employment status, poverty status, level of trust in the medical provider, English as native language, and insurance status. Second, this study examined a series of nine health-related beliefs by matching status. These health-related beliefs examined patient views of health services, access to services, and patient and physician roles in recovery from illness.

Data analyses consisted of a series of cross-tabulations between variables of interest and match/nonmatch status. The data analysis program, SUDAAN, was used to conduct these analyses. Actual cell-wise counts generated by these cross-tabulations served as the data used to conduct tests of significance. However, for ease of inspection, data in tables 1.1 and 1.2 are presented as percentages within the match and nonmatch categories. For each analysis, chi-square

(χ^2) was the statistic used to evaluate the strength of association between levels for each variable of interest and its matching status.

RESULTS

Table 1.1 presents patient background characteristics by matched and nonmatched status separately for African American and for Hispanic patients. These results are based on a total sample of 3,562 African American patients, including 363 patient-physician matched pairs and 3,199 nonmatched pairs. For Hispanics, the total number of cases was 1,777, with 258 patient-physician matched pairs and 1,519 nonmatches.

Patient Background by Matching Status

For African Americans, there were no significant differences between patient-physician matches and nonmatches on the patient characteristics of self-rating of health, poverty status, trust of medical providers, and English as native language; that is, these patient characteristics were independent of matching status. Among African Americans, English was identified as their native language in over 97 percent of the cases in both the matched and nonmatched conditions.

In contrast to Hispanics, the distribution of cases for African Americans differed for the matches relative to the nonmatches on marital status, employment status, and insurance status. Regarding marital status, larger proportions of the matched cases were separated, divorced, or widowed compared with the nonmatched cases. Regarding employment status, a higher proportion of the matched cases were unemployed (39.1%) than employed (30.9%), and this difference was significant ($\chi^2 = 8.64$, $p < .01$). Regarding insurance status, a larger proportion of the matched cases had public insurance (26.2%) compared with the nonmatched cases (16.3%). By contrast, a higher proportion of the nonmatches were uninsured (17.9%) compared to the matched cases (11.9%). Across the four insurance categories, the distribution of cases for the matched group was significantly different from the distribution of cases among the nonmatched group ($\chi^2 = 27.33$, $p < 0001$). In other words, among African Americans, type of insurance coverage or lack of coverage was associated with matching status.

For Hispanics, there were *no* differences between the matched and nonmatched status on the patient characteristics of self-rating of health, marital status, and insurance status. By contrast, significant differences in the distribution of cases were observed on the patient variables of employment status, poverty status, trust of medical providers, and English as native language. Thus, there was an association between these variables and matching status.

Regarding English as native language, Hispanics, as expected, exhibited a pattern distinct from that of African Americans. Among African Americans, native language was independent of matching status. Under both matching categories, English was the native language for over 97 percent of the cases. By contrast, for Hispanics, only 21.3 percent of cases identified English as a native language under the matched condition, while 39 percent of nonmatched did ($\chi^2 = 29.67$, $p < .01$). This indicates that among the patient-physician matches, a lower proportion had English as their native language than did nonmatches. This suggests that Hispanics who did not have English as their native language (78.7 percent of the matched cases) may have looked for a physician who was able to speak Spanish or who was Hispanic in background.

In other comparisons of patient-physician matches versus non-matches among Hispanics, the matched cases exhibited a higher proportion of unemployment (34.6%) compared with the nonmatches (27.4%), a higher proportion of matched patients lived above poverty status (89.5%) compared with nonmatched patients (84.0%), and a higher proportion of matches expressed a high level of trust in their physician (49.6%) compared with nonmatches (38.6%).

Health-Related Beliefs by Matching Status

Table 1.2 presents patient health-related beliefs by matching status. Nine items that examine patient beliefs about health care, the role of the physician, the patient's views on his own health care, and insurance coverage were examined across matching status. For African Americans, all of these patient health-related beliefs were independent of matching status. By contrast, for Hispanics seven of the nine items were associated with matching status. For Hispanics, only two items showed no difference across the matched and nonmatched conditions: "I am too healthy to need insurance" and "Health insurance is not worth the cost."

Among Hispanics, the item, "Care is easily available without cash," exhibited a significant difference across levels of matching status ($\chi^2 = 12.88$, $p < .01$) As shown in table 1.2, a higher proportion of matched patients agreed but also a higher proportion disagreed, leaving a lower proportion that was undecided on the ease of availability of health care without cash. For the item, "One's own behavior determines recovery," more matched cases than unmatched cases disagreed ($\chi^2 = 10.77$, $p < .01$). This suggests that relative to nonmatched patients, matched patients believed more strongly that the physician is an important factor in determining recovery from illness. For the item, "Doctors only recommend necessary surgery," a higher proportion of matched than nonmatched patients agreed (60.3% versus 48.4%; $\chi^2 = 12.95$, $p < .01$). These results suggest that Hispanic matched patients, relative to the nonmatched patients, were more likely to believe that the physician will make a correct medical decision for them. This result corroborates the stronger level of trust in the medical provider expressed by matched patients in the previous analyses of patient background characteristics.

Four items in this set examined self-care issues, including the role of luck in recovery. For the item, "Luck may be part of recovery," only a small proportion of patients in both conditions believed that luck affects recovery, although a higher proportion of matched patients agreed in the role of luck in recovery from illness (13.4% versus 12.8%; $\chi^2 = 9.60$, $p < .05$). Similarly, for the item, "I know my own health better than the doctor does," a higher proportion of the matched Hispanic cases disagreed (54.3% versus 44.2%; $\chi^2 = 10.19$, $p < .05$). This response indicates that the Hispanic matched patients attributed greater knowledge about their own health to the physician than to themselves. Similarly, for the item, "I can get well without the doctor," a higher proportion of the matched patients disagreed (55.7% versus 42.6%; $\chi^2 = 13.91$, $p < .01$). Here also the matched Hispanic patients expressed a greater trust in the physician's curative skills, perhaps along with greater dependence on the physician. Paradoxically, for the item, "Home remedies are better than medical treatment," a higher proportion of Hispanic matched patients agreed with this statement (34.0% versus 30.8%; $\chi^2 = 8.35$, $p < .05$). Interestingly, although more Hispanic matched patients than nonmatched patients endorsed the importance of the physician in aiding recovery from illness, the matched patients also seemed to endorse more strongly the belief that home remedies are better than medical treatment. Despite this observed relative difference by matching status, the greater proportion of respondents overall endorsed the view that medical treatment is indeed superior to home remedies.

DISCUSSION

The results of these analyses examining patient-physician matches compared to nonmatches for African Americans and for Hispanics yielded several significant associations between health-related beliefs and matching status among Hispanics, but not among African Americans. Since, for Hispanics, matching status was also associated with language, employment status, and poverty status, the patterns observed between health-related beliefs and matching status could also have been influenced, in part, by these other background variables. As indicated in table 1.1, a major patient background characteristic associated with matching status among Hispanics was language, although clearly language was not associated with matching status among African Americans. Hispanics indicated that English was not their native language in 78.7 percent of cases among the matched patients and in 61 percent of cases in the nonmatched condition. Among Hispanics, having Spanish as their native language might underlie the series of differences in health-related beliefs observed for matched Hispanic patients relative to unmatched Hispanic patients. While patient-physician similarity in ethnic/racial background may be an important variable in establishing a sound doctor-patient relationship, the present study suggests that for many Hispanics, speaking Spanish only, either currently or in the past, is another important factor associated with matching status. While temporal or causal relations cannot be ascertained from these cross-sectional data, one might surmise that Hispanic patients who have not developed proficiency in English must actively seek out physicians who understand Spanish, often leading them to find a Hispanic physician. Of course, beyond language, it is likely that these Hispanic patients, especially those who speak only Spanish, would want to have a physician who understands them not only in terms of verbal statements but also in terms of cultural issues that are expressed in language and in a system of beliefs about health and illness.

The various differences in health-related beliefs observed for matched Hispanic patients relative to nonmatched Hispanic patients suggest that for Hispanic matched patients, the physician is seen as credible and capable of offering sound care in illness recovery. These patients also endorsed the importance of the physician for aid in recovery from illness, which was not seen as easily attainable by the patient's own efforts at self-care. While these patterns of belief suggest orientation toward an external locus of control among the Hispanic matched patients, a more cogent explanation may involve their willingness to trust and confide in the physician.

By contrast, it is noteworthy that beliefs involving insurance coverage were independent of matching status among Hispanics and African Americans. (Table 1.2) Among members of both ethnic/racial groups, insurance was believed to be essential to accessing health care. For Hispanics, this is a particularly important issue since large proportions of Hispanics, particularly Mexican Americans, find themselves without adequate insurance coverage, a fact that constitutes a major barrier to health-care access (Ginzberg 1991).

CONCLUSIONS AND POLICY IMPLICATIONS

These results have interesting policy implications. First, they indicate that certain health-related beliefs about the role of the patient and of the physician in recovery from illness are associated with patient-physician matching status in Hispanics, but not in African Americans. For both groups, health insurance is an important resource that patients themselves deem crucial for maintaining health. By contrast, it is unclear why matching status in the African American group was unrelated to the health-related beliefs about the working relationship between patient and physician. This is not to say that matching by racial/ethnic background is not important, as a relationship may exist among African Americans between patient-physician matching status and other variables, such as health outcome, which were not included in this study. For example, in the aforementioned relationship between matching status and health insurance coverage, 26.2 percent of African American patients with a physician of the same racial background (the matched group) had Medicaid (public insurance) compared with only 16.3 percent of the African American patients in the nonmatched group. This finding indicates either that African Americans with Medicaid coverage are more comfortable with physicians of their own race, or else that physicians of other racial groups are less available to African Americans with Medicaid.

By contrast, for many Hispanics, it appears that language may have operated as a significant mediating variable. Especially among monolingual Spanish-speaking patients, the need for a same-culture physician-patient match would likely motivate seeking a physician of one's "own kind," a physician who is able to communicate adequately in Spanish and who understands one's health needs within a Hispanic cultural context.

The policy implications of these findings include the great need for more physicians who are able to communicate adequately with Hispanics. Ideally, this would include larger numbers of both Spanish-speaking Hispanic physicians and non-Hispanic physicians who understand the language and the culture of the Hispanic patient. Unfortunately, the rate at which new Hispanic physicians are being trained is low, thus prompting the need to increase the number of non-Hispanic physicians who are able to speak Spanish and understand the beliefs, attitudes, and orientation to health care of Hispanic patients. In other words, this suggests the need for *cultural competence training* for all physicians. This would involve in-depth training on the cultural aspects of health care for Hispanics to enhance the physician's capacity to work effectively with various Hispanic patients, as though they were culturally matched.

In the present study, matching status was not associated with various health-related beliefs among African Americans. However, it was associated with two important economic resource variables—employment status and insurance coverage—that may be proxies for other health-related variables. For this reason, the existence of such a relationship can't be ruled out entirely. Thus cultural competency training for physicians who work with African Americans also would be appropriate. This need would be accentuated if a future study of African Americans finds an association between matching status and actual health outcomes. For example, among African Americans, is patient-physician matching associated with greater patient compliance when taking medications for high blood pressure and with actual blood pressure control at normal levels? In conclusion, the results of the present study provide preliminary evidence about the importance of cultural matches between patients and physicians as these matches relate to certain patient health-related beliefs about the role of the patient and the physician in health and in recovery from illness.

References

Andersen, R., S. Lewis, and A. Giachello. 1981. Access to medical care among the Hispanic population of the Southwestern United States. *Journal of Health and Social Behavior* 22:78-89.

Castro, F.G., E. Barrington, E. Sharp, L. Dial, B. Wang, and R. Rawson. 1992. Behavioral and psychological profiles of cocaine users upon treatment entry: Ethnic comparisons. *Drugs and Society* 17:231-251.

Castro, F.G., P. Furth, and H. Karlow. 1984. The health beliefs of Mexican, Mexican American, and Anglo American women. *Hispanic Journal of Behavioral Sciences* 6:365-383.

Council on Scientific Affairs. 1991. Hispanic health in the United States. *Journal of the American Medical Association* 265:248-252.

Dana, R.H. 1993. *Multicultural Assessment Perspectives for Professional Psychology.* Boston: Allyn and Bacon.

de la Cancela, V. 1992. Keeping African-American and Latino males alive: Policy and program initiatives in health. *Journal of Multi-Cultural Community Health* 2:31-39.

Elder, J., F.G. Castro, C. Moor, J. Mayer, J. Candelaria, N. Campbell, G. Talavera, and L. Ware. 1991. Differences in cancer-risk-related behaviors in Latino and Anglo adults. *Preventive Medicine* 20:751-763.

Flaskerud, J., and H. Li-tze. 1992. Racial/ethnic identity and amount and type of psychiatric treatment. *American Journal of Psychiatry* 149:379-384.

Giachello, A.L.M. 1994. Issues of access and use. In *Latino Health in the U.S.: A Growing Challenge,* edited by C.W. Molina and M. Aguirre-Molina, 83-111. Washington, DC: American Public Health Association.

Ginzberg, E. 1991. Access to health care for Hispanics. *Journal of the American Medical Association* 265:238-241.

Gomez, R., P. Ruiz, and R. Rumbaut. 1985. Hispanic patients: A linguo-cultural minority. *Hispanic Journal of Behavioral Sciences* 7:177-186.

Haffner, S., H. Hazuda, B. Mitchell, J. Patterson, and M. Stern. 1991. Increased incidence of type II diabetes mellitus in Mexican Americans. *Diabetes Care* 14:102-108.

Hale, C.B. 1992. A demographic profile of African Americans. In *Health Issues in the Black Community,* edited by R.L. Braithwaite and S.E.Taylor, 6-19. San Francisco: Jossey-Bass.

Harper, A.C., and L.J. Lambert. 1994. *The Health of Populations: An Introduction*, 2nd ed. New York: Springer.

Harwood, A. 1981. Guidelines for culturally appropriate health care. In *Ethnicity and Medical Care*, edited by A. Harwood. Cambridge, MA: Harvard University Press.

Leaf, P., M. Bruce, G. Tischler, and C. Holzer. 1987. The relationship between demographic factors and attitudes toward mental health services. *Journal of Community Psychology* 15:275-284.

Lewin-Epstein, N. 1991. Determinants of regular source of health care in Black, Mexican, Puerto Rican, and non-Hispanic white populations. *Medical Care* 29:543-557.

Montgomery, P.A. 1994. *The Hispanic Population in the United States: March 1993*. Current Population Reports, P20-475. Washington, DC: U.S. Bureau of the Census.

Orlandi, M.A. 1992. The challenge of evaluating community-based prevention programs: A cross-cultural perspective. In *Cultural Competence for Evaluators*, edited by M.A. Orlandi, R. Weston, and L.G. Epstein, 1-22. Rockville, MD: US Department of Health and Human Services, Public Health Service.

Pinderhughes, E. 1982. Afro-American families and the victim system. In *Ethnicity and Family Therapy*, edited by M. McGoldrick, J.K. Pearce, and J. Giordano, 108-122. New York: Guilford.

Quesada, G., and P. Heller. 1977. Sociocultural barriers to medical care among Mexican Americans in Texas: A summary report to research conducted by the Southwest Medical Sociological Ad Hoc Committee. *Medical Care* 15:93-100.

Roter, D., J. Hall, and N. Katz. 1988. Patient-physician communication: A descriptive summary of the literature. *Patient Education and Counseling* 12:99.

Treviño, F.M., M.E. Moyer, R.B. Valdez, and C.A. Stroup-Benham. 1992. Health insurance coverage and underutilization of health services by Mexican Americans, Puerto Ricans, and Cuban Americans. In *Health Policy and the Hispanic*, edited by A. Furnio, 158-170. Boulder, CO: Westview.

Walker, B. 1992. Health policies and the black community. In *Health Issues in the Black Community*, edited by R.L. Braithwaite and S.E. Taylor, 315-320. San Francisco: Jossey-Bass.

Wells, K., R. Hough, J. Golding, A. Burnam, and M. Karno. 1987. Which Mexican-Americans underutilized health services? *American Journal of Psychiatry* 144:918-922.

Westbrook, K., B. Brown, and C. McBride. 1975. Breast cancer: A critical review of a patient sample with a ten-year follow up. *Southern Medical Journal* 58:543-548.

White, J.L., and T.A. Parham. 1990. *The Psychology of Blacks: An African American Perspective*, 2nd ed. Englewood Cliffs, NJ: Prentice Hall.

Table 1.1
Patient/physician matches by patient characteristics and race/ethnicity, 1987
(In percents)

	AFRICAN AMERICANS			HISPANICS		
	Matches N=363	Nonmatches N=3,199	χ^2	Matches N=258	Nonmatches N=1,519	χ^2
SELF-RATING OF HEALTH			5.61			4.03
Excellent	18.7	23.1		20.9	26.6	
Good	54.0	52.9		53.1	50.6	
Fair	24.0	20.0		22.5	19.5	
Poor	3.3	4.0		3.5	3.4	
MARITAL STATUS			10.80*			1.32
Never married	27.0	34.7		21.8	23.7	
Married	41.8	41.3		60.4	60.4	
Separated	9.5	7.9		4.5	4.0	
Divorced	15.5	11.5		9.4	9.0	
Widowed	6.2	4.6		4.0	2.7	
EMPLOYMENT STATUS			8.64**			4.37*
Employed	60.9	69.1		65.4	72.6	
Unemployed	39.1	30.9		34.6	27.4	
POVERTY STATUS			3.11			5.24*
Above	78.8	82.5		89.5	84.0	
At or below	21.2	17.5		10.5	16.0	
TRUST OF MEDICAL PROVIDER			2.74			10.04**
High	47.7	44.2		49.6	38.6	
Medium	35.4	40.1		35.9	43.4	
Low	16.9	15.7		14.5	18.0	
ENGLISH IS NATIVE LANGUAGE			3.79			29.67**
Yes	97.2	98.6		21.3	39.0	
No	2.8	1.4		78.7	61.0	

Continued on next page

Table 1.1 continued

	AFRICAN AMERICANS			HISPANICS		
	Matches N=363	Nonmatches N=3,199	χ^2	Matches N=258	Nonmatches N=1,519	χ^2
INSURANCE STATUS			27.33***			3.44
Private	45.7	46.4		38.4	41.6	
Public	26.2	16.3		15.1	12.2	
Uninsured	11.9	17.9		24.8	22.0	
Unknown	16.3	19.4		21.7	24.2	

SOURCE: 1987 National Medical Expenditure Survey
NOTE: Percents may not sum to 100 due to rounding.
$^*p < 0.05$ $^{**}p < 0.01$ $^{***}p < 0.001$

Table 1.2
Patient/physician matches by patient health-related beliefs and race/ethnicity, 1987
(In percents)

	AFRICAN AMERICANS			HISPANICS		
	Matches N=363	Nonmatches N=3,199	χ^2	Matches N=258	Nonmatches N=1,519	χ^2
CARE IS EASILY AVAILABLE WITHOUT CASH.			4.52			12.88**
Agree	24.1	20.2		27.5	24.2	
Neither	12.4	14.1		10.7	16.4	
Disagree	63.6	65.6		61.8	59.4	
ONE'S OWN BEHAVIOR DETERMINES RECOVERY.			6.14			10.77**
Agree	51.7	52.5		42.7	53.4	
Neither	10.8	13.5		20.3	17.2	
Disagree	37.5	34.0		37.1	29.4	
DOCTORS ONLY RECOMMEND NECESSARY SURGERY.			6.17			12.95**
Agree	50.2	46.0		60.3	48.4	
Neither	15.5	20.1		17.7	20.9	
Disagree	34.4	33.9		22.0	30.7	
LUCK MAY BE PART OF RECOVERY.			4.89			9.60*
Agree	13.0	12.8		13.4	12.8	
Neither	8.7	12.6		15.6	17.1	
Disagree	78.3	74.6		71.0	70.2	
I KNOW MY OWN HEALTH BETTER THAN THE DOCTOR.			2.41			10.19*
Agree	41.9	39.2		32.5	38.0	
Neither	10.3	12.4		13.3	17.8	
Disagree	47.8	48.4		54.3	44.2	

Continued on next page

Table 1.2 continued

	AFRICAN AMERICANS			HISPANICS		
	Matches $N=363$	Nonmatches $N=3,199$	χ^2	Matches $N=258$	Nonmatches $N=1,519$	χ^2
I CAN GET WELL WITHOUT THE DOCTOR.			0.71			13.91**
Agree	41.1	42.9		33.5	44.9	
Neither	10.2	10.7		10.9	12.4	
Disagree	49.6	46.4		55.7	42.6	
HOME REMEDIES ARE BETTER THAN MEDICAL TREATMENT.			5.74			8.35*
Agree	31.2	31.5		34.0	30.8	
Neither	13.9	17.5		16.4	19.8	
Disagree	54.9	51.1		49.6	49.4	
I AM TOO HEALTHY TO NEED INSURANCE.			2.32			1.30
Agree	10.5	10.6		19.0	18.5	
Neither	9.9	10.9		14.7	16.8	
Disagree	79.6	78.4		66.4	64.7	
HEALTH INSURANCE IS NOT WORTH THE COST.			4.57			7.90
Agree	21.6	19.5		19.7	23.5	
Neither	17.3	14.1		18.4	20.5	
Disagree	61.1	66.4		62.1	56.0	

SOURCE: 1987 National Medical Expenditure Survey
NOTE: Percents may not sum to 100 due to rounding.
*$p < 0.05$ **$p < 0.01$

Social, Economic, and Health Determinants of the Use of Health Care Services by Whites, African Americans, and Mexican Americans

Verna M. Keith and Thomas A. LaVeist

Racial and ethnic differences in access to health care declined significantly during the 1960s and 1970s. Indeed, numerous reports and studies suggested that racial/ethnic minority populations had attained parity with the non-Hispanic white population in both physician and hospital use (Aday, Andersen, and Fleming 1980; Adey, Fleming, and Andersen 1984; Andersen, Lion, and Anderson 1976). Recent research, however, suggests a reversal in the trend toward racial/ethnic convergence. Nationwide studies conducted in the 1980s indicate that, compared to whites, African Americans and Hispanics are less likely to visit a physician and more likely to encounter barriers to needed medical care (Blendon et al. 1989; Hayward et al. 1988; Cornelius 1993).

These recent studies have made an important contribution by drawing attention to the problems experienced by African Americans and Hispanics in gaining access to the health-care system. However, if these inequities are to be addressed, researchers must identify factors that enhance or restrict access to care within each racial/ ethnic group. Research of this type is especially critical given that the lack of access to appropriate and timely health services may contribute to continuing higher morbidity and mortality rates among minority populations (Council on Scientific Affairs 1991; Nickens 1991; US DHHS 1985).

Over the past several decades, researchers have identified a number of factors that affect the use of health services, including health insurance coverage, health status, access to a regular source of care, and type of provider (Andersen, Lion, and Anderson 1976; Aday, Andersen, and Fleming 1980; Aday, Fleming, and Andersen; Aday, Fleming, and Andersen 1984; Dutton 1978). Other researchers have noted that belief in the efficacy of medical care and other health-related attitudes are important determinants of use (Berkanovic, Telesky, and Reeder 1981; Berkanovic and Telesky 1985; Langlie 1977). A comprehensive assessment of how these factors affect current utilization patterns among minority populations has not been undertaken.

To address this issue, this study investigates the contributions of social, economic, and health status to the use of health services among non-Hispanic whites, African Americans, and Mexican Americans. For each group, the effects of use patterns on socioeconomic status, availability and type of insurance coverage, availability and type of regular provider, attitudes toward medical care, and health status are assessed separately, using multivariate statistical techniques. Mexican Americans are the only Hispanic subpopulation analyzed because small sample sizes preclude separate analyses for the remaining Hispanic groups. While "all other Hispanics" could be aggregated into a single category, this does not seem informative given the social, economic, and health-related differences among Cubans, Puerto Ricans, and others.

Because past studies gave often gave considerable weight to attitudes in explaining racial and class differences, we are especially interested in assessing the extent to which attitudes toward medical care continue to predict use (Berkanovic and Reeder 1974; Stahl and Gardner 1976; Suchman 1965). This research enhances our understanding of racial/ethnic differences in use of health care and identifies African Americans, Mexican Americans, and whites who have the most difficulty in acquiring services.

USE OF HEALTH SERVICES BY AFRICAN AMERICANS

Prior to the 1970s, the findings from national surveys indicated that "nonwhites," 95 percent of whom were African American, were less likely than whites to visit a physician, to be hospitalized, or to have preventive checkups (Aday and Eichorn 1972; Jackson 1980). Racial differences in place of treatment and type of provider were especially striking. African Americans were more likely than white Americans to be treated in hospital outpatient clinics and emergency rooms and less likely to see a physician in his or her private office (Aday and Eichorn 1972). The differences were generally attributed to economic disadvantages, less health insurance coverage, lower primary care physician-to-population ratios in the African American community, and negative attitudes toward the health-care delivery system, resulting in delayed help-seeking.

After the passage of Medicare and Medicaid in the mid 1960s, racial differences in the use of health services narrowed markedly (Aday, Andersen, and Fleming 1980; Aday, Fleming, and Andersen 1984; Benham and Benham 1975). In 1970, for example, 42 percent of African Americans had no physician visits compared with 30 percent of whites (Andersen, Lion, and Anderson 1976). By 1982, just under 20 percent of both whites and African Americans reported not seeing a physician. In 1970, the average annual number of physician visits was 4.1 for whites compared to 3.6 for African Americans. This differential had been reduced to a 0.2 gap in annual visits by 1978-1980 (Treviño and Moss 1984). The differential in hospitalization rates also was virtually eliminated during this period. Although morbidity profiles suggest that African Americans should have exceeded whites in physician use and hospitalization, just attaining parity on these indicators represented a remarkable achievement.

After two decades of progress, however, disparities in the use of physician services by whites and African Americans appear to have re-emerged. Based on a national survey conducted in 1986, Blendon and colleagues (1989) report that 37.2 percent of African Americans compared to 31.7 percent of whites did not see a physician in the year prior to the survey. These differentials remain when the sample is stratified by health status. In fact, larger racial disparities occur among those in fair or poor health, the population in greatest need of services. Cornelius (1993) also reports similar findings for physician access based on data from the 1987 National Medical Expenditure Survey (NMES). Further, Hayward et al. (1988) found that even among insured, working-age adults, African Americans are more likely to report that they are unable to obtain needed supportive medical services, medications, or supplies. Among those with a chronic medical condition, African Americans are also 1.7 times as likely as whites not to have visited a physician. Together with longstanding racial inequities in the place of service and in the use of preventive services, these findings indicate that a re-evaluation of access to health care among African Americans is urgently needed.

USE OF HEALTH SERVICES BY HISPANICS

An adequate assessment of long-term trends in the use of health services among Hispanics is complicated by several factors. Until 1976, government agencies classified Hispanics as white, a practice that precluded access to information on morbidity and on the use of services. Over the years, federal agencies and researchers also have used varying criteria to define Hispanic ethnicity (e.g., Spanish surname versus self-designated ethnic identity), making it difficult to compare findings and to assess trends. Some studies have been confined to Hispanic groups in a particular geographical area or, if based on a national survey, have not reported findings separately for specific groups (Treviño et al. 1991).

The limited data available suggest that access to health care became more difficult for Hispanics in the eighties just as it did for African Americans. Among Hispanics, utilization rates as well as socioeconomic status differ on the basis of national origin (e.g., Mexican Americans versus Cubans) (US Bureau of the Census 1993). Based on 1978-1980 data, Treviño and Moss (1984) reported few racial/ethnic differences in physician use, although after disaggregating the data Mexican Americans were clearly disadvantaged relative to other Hispanic and non-Hispanic groups. Data collected in 1982 by Andersen, Giachello, and Aday (1986) also revealed only a 2 percentage point difference in the proportion not seeing a physician, 20 percent for whites and 18 percent for Hispanics. However, by the late eighties, 41 percent of Hispanics versus 27 percent of whites reported not seeing a physician (Cornelius 1993). Similar to findings comparing African American and whites, Hayward and colleagues (1988) also report that working-age Hispanics with chronic or serious medical conditions are twice as likely as similar whites not to visit a physician. Both studies examined physician contact by health status, health insurance coverage, and other factors affecting use of services, but neither assessed the relative importance of these determinants. Moreover, neither study disaggregated the Hispanic population, so knowledge of the Mexican-American population is severely lacking.

DETERMINANTS OF HEALTH CARE USE

A massive body of research has documented a relationship between use of health services and a number of social, economic, and health status factors. For example, use is greater among the elderly, females, those who rate their health as poor, and those reporting a regular source of care (Aday, Andersen, and Fleming 1980; Aday, Fleming, and Andersen 1984; Andersen, Lion, and Anderson 1976; Blendon et al. 1989). Insurance coverage also is critical for accessing services in a timely manner. The uninsured not only report fewer physician visits, but also tend to be sicker at the time of hospitalization and are more likely to die before being discharged (Kleinman, Gold, and Markuc 1981; Newacheck 1988; Hadley, Steinberg, and Feder 1991; Weissman et al. 1991). It is also well documented that many of these factors differ among racial/ethnic groups. Hispanic and African American communities are younger and have fewer economic resources than white communities. Compared to whites, Hispanics and African Americans are significantly less likely to have health insurance coverage (Blendon et al. 1989; Cornelius 1993). Mexican Americans are the least likely to be covered by any type of insurance (Treviño et al. 1991).

Both Hispanics and African Americans are still less likely to have a regular source of care than whites and are more dependent upon hospital outpatient departments and emergency rooms for medical care (Cornelius 1993). Compared to other groups, Mexican Americans are the least likely to have a regular source of care (Treviño et al. 1991). It is generally agreed that continuity of care becomes more difficult when hospital facilities are the primary site for service delivery. Poor health, one of the strongest predictors of service use, is also reported more frequently by Hispanics and African Americans than by whites (Cornelius 1993; Treviño et al. 1991).

One line of research has also emphasized the importance of beliefs and attitudes about health and health care in determining patterns of use and has been used extensively to account for racial and social

31

class differences. Indeed, Dutton (1978) noted the strong tendency to portray beliefs and attitudes as being more salient than other barriers to care such as type of provider. Research based on this perspective suggests that socially and economically disadvantaged groups such as the poor and ethnic minorities are less likely to use health services because they are more skeptical of medical services and less knowledgeable about appropriate health behavior (Becker et al. 1977; Berkanovic and Reeder 1974; Wolinsky 1982). It is generally argued that these attitudes represent cultural traditions or have developed in response to financial and social constraints to seeking medical care (Rundall and Wheeler 1979; Sharp, Ross, and Cockerham 1983). This perspective remains prominent although research by Dutton (1978) and Rundall and Wheeler (1979) convincingly argues that characteristics of the delivery system are more important than cultural traits in explaining class and race differences in use.

Racial/ethnic and social class differences in attitudes toward medical care appear to have narrowed over the past decade and may even have changed. Berkanovic and Telesky (1985) found that belief in the efficacy of medical care affects help-seeking among whites as well as among African Americans and Mexican Americans. Sharp, Ross, and Cockerham (1983), on the other hand, reported that African Americans hold more positive attitudes toward visiting a physician than do whites. These authors speculate that African American attitudes became more positive as Medicare and Medicaid reduced financial barriers which, in turn, increased their access to the health-care system. With respect to class differences in attitudes, data presented by Haug and Lavin (1981, 1983) show that it is better-educated persons, rather than those with low educational attainment, who are now more skeptical about physicians. These researchers argue for a growing trend toward consumerism in the practitioner-patient relationship whereby higher status persons desire greater responsibility in managing their health and feel less inclined to entrust all health-care decisions to physicians. Sharp, Ross, and Cockerham (1983) suggest a similar process may be occurring among racial groups, with African Americans becoming less skeptical and whites more skeptical. Taken together, this body of research indicates that attitudes and beliefs remain important predictors of health-care use but may be less important for understanding racial/ethnic differences than they were in previous decades.

DATA AND METHODS

The study uses data from the Household Survey component of the 1987 NMES (see Appendix.) The survey, which used a stratified multistage area probability design, oversampled minority populations, the poor, persons with functional disabilities, and the elderly. Information was gathered on health-care use, expenditures, health insurance coverage, and sociodemographic characteristics. Respondents were also asked to complete a self-administered questionnaire on subjective health status, availability and type of regular source of care, and attitudes toward medical care. This study was limited to adults 25 to 64 years old at the time of the first interview. Within this age range, approximately 9,775 persons identified themselves as white, 2,830 identified themselves as African American, and 810 identified themselves as Mexican American.

Dependent Variables

Three indicators of health services use are analyzed in the study: (1) blood pressure check, (2) ambulatory contact, and (3) number of ambulatory visits among those with a contact. *Blood pressure check* in the past year is a dichotomous variable used as an indicator of access to preventive health services. Having a blood pressure check is regarded as a preventive practice because the timely diagnosis of hypertension lowers the risk of more serious medical conditions including heart disease, stroke, and end-stage renal failure. Further, diagnosed hypertensives also should have their blood pressure monitored periodically to avoid these critical medical problems.

Ambulatory contact is a dichotomous variable indicating whether the respondent had any contact, either in person or by telephone, with hospital emergency rooms, hospital outpatient departments, private physicians, nurses, or any other health-care providers. Ambulatory contact indicates whether respondents were successful in gaining access to the health-care delivery system. The reference period is during the past year.

Mean number of ambulatory visits for those with at least one contact during the previous year is used to assess number of visits. This measure is preferable to mean number of visits by all persons surveyed because it does not average in those who were unable to access the system. To avoid giving disproportionate weight to frequent users, this variable is truncated at 10 visits or higher. This decision was based on past research with the National Health Interview Survey.

Independent Variables

Two indicators of socioeconomic status are used in the analyses—educational attainment and poverty status. *Education* is measured as years of school completed and ranges from no years of schooling (0) to six years of college or more (18). *Poverty status*, a measure based on annual family income and family size, indicates economic position relative to the poverty line. This variable is coded as a set of dummy variables with the following categories: poor—under 100 percent of poverty; near-poor—100 to 149 percent of poverty; and nonpoor—150 percent of poverty or above. Persons with incomes between 150 percent and 200 percent of the poverty line, known in some research as low-income, were grouped with the nonpoor for practical and conceptual reasons. First, given the sample size limitations for the Mexican Americans, the number of independent variables had to be limited. In this case, the number of possible dummy variables was reduced from five to three. Second, it was deemed undesirable to group near-poor and low-income persons because any findings for the near-poor would be obscured. The near-poor are a notch group that may have a particularly difficult problem in accessing health care. For example, among the uninsured, 36 percent are near-poor while 28 percent are low-income (Employee Benefit Research Institute 1994). Thus, since the number of variables had to be limited, the near-poor was kept as a separate category because of its relevance to policy considerations.

Availability and type of insurance coverage is measured by creating a set of dummy variables with three categories: private—includes coverage by some form of private insurance; public—includes coverage by public sources such as Medicaid, Medicare, CHAMPUS, CHAMPVA, and other public assistance; uninsured—no coverage by private or public sources.

Availability and type of regular provider is measured by creating a set of dummy variables that combine whether respondents have a regular source and a regular place of care. The created variables are as follows: private—includes usual source of care in private doctor's office or group practice and doctor's clinic; non-private—includes usual source of care in hospital outpatient clinics, emergency rooms, walk-in centers, and all other nonprivate sources; and no regular provider/no regular source of care.

Health status, an indicator of need for health care, is measured by asking respondents to rate their health from "1" excellent to "4" poor. For the analyses of blood pressure, a dichotomous variable measuring the presence of hypertension is also included.

Skepticism is measured by a five-item attitude scale that reflects level of confidence in the medical profession's understanding of and ability to intervene in illness efficaciously. The five items (each with a 5-point response ranging from "disagree strongly" to "agree strongly") were: (1) "I can overcome most illness without help from a medically trained professional," (2) "Home remedies are often better than drugs prescribed by a doctor," (3) "If I get sick, it is my own behavior that determines how soon I get well," (4) "I understand my health better than most doctors do," and (5) "Luck plays a big part in determining how soon I will recover from an illness." Higher scores indicate a more skeptical attitude. Since skepticism can be interpreted as the opposite of a belief in efficacy, the items selected for the skepticism scale are similar to the measures of efficacy used by Berkanovic, Telesky, and Reeder (1981) who factor-analyzed a number of health beliefs. It is important to note that the measure of skepticism used in this report does not indicate whether respondents are skeptical because they are: (1) self-reliant and thus believe that they can take care of themselves, especially if medical symptoms do not seem to pose a serious threat; or (2) fatalistic and believe that recovery from symptoms is a matter of luck or fate. Thus, either scenario could underlie high levels of skepticism. Unfortunately, there is no way to untangle this effect given the data at hand.

Sociodemographic variables include: age, measured in years, and sex, measured as a dummy variable (1 for females and 0 for males). A set of dummy variables measuring rural-urban residence is also created as follows: large SMSA (Standard Metropolitan Statistical Area)—residence in the 19 largest Smsas; small SMSA—residence in a smaller SMSA; and non-SMSA—residence in a nonmetropolitan area.

Analyses

Logistic regression techniques are used in the analyses of the dichotomous dependent variables—blood pressure check and ambulatory contact—in the past year. Ordinary least squares regression is used in the analysis of number of ambulatory visits among those with at least one contact. Each regression equation is estimated separately for whites, African Americans, and Mexican Americans to permit assessment of the relative importance of the independent variables within each group. Because NMES is a complex survey design, the statistical package SUDAAN is used to obtain accurate estimates of the standard errors for all results presented below. Although skepticism is not the primary dependent variable under investigation in this study, it is especially significant to the analyses of the utilization measures. Therefore, as a preliminary step, we examine factors related to skepticism within each racial/ethnic group. We then turn to the analyses of health-care utilization measures.

Factors Related to Skepticism

Table 2.1 presents bivariate relationships between skepticism and selected financial and medical variables for whites, African Americans, and Mexican Americans. For purposes of these descriptive analyses, skepticism has been categorized as low (1–12), medium (13–17), and high (18–25). Chi-square (χ^2) is used to indicate whether the bivariate relationships are significant. It should be noted that χ^2 is very sensitive to large sample size. Thus, in sample sizes of several thousand respondents very weak effects can be statistically significant but substantively meaningless. Given the sample sizes of the three racial/ethnic groups, results should be interpreted with caution, especially those for whites who number more than 9,000. Gamma (γ) indicates the direction and strength of a relationship and ranges from -1.00 to +1.00. A γ coefficient of -.46, for example, indicates that the relationship is negative and of moderate strength, while a γ of .10 indicates that the relationship is positive and represents a weak association (Davis 1971).

RESULTS

Table 2.1 reveals that among whites the poor and near-poor are more likely to be skeptical of medical care, although the γ coefficient indicates that the relationship is weak. The overall proportions of whites, African Americans, and Mexican Americans that were highly skeptical of medical care were 15 percent, 14 percent, and 16 percent, respectively (data not shown). Among African Americans and Mexican Americans, however, the nonpoor are slightly more likely to be skeptical of medical care. Generally, the relationship is quite weak for both minority groups. For all three racial/ethnic groups, insurance status and availability and type of provider are negatively associated with skepticism. Among whites, the uninsured and those with public insurance tend to be more skeptical than those with private insurance, and those with no regular provider are more skeptical than those with either a nonprivate or private provider. Among African Americans and Mexican Americans, the uninsured are most skeptical, but there is little difference between those with public and private insurance. For both minority populations, those with no regular provider have the highest degree of skepticism, with practically no difference between those with nonprivate and private providers. On the other hand, skepticism is positively related to health status for all groups, with those in excellent health most doubtful of the efficacy of medical care. The relationship is especially strong among Mexican Americans, as indicated by the γ coefficient.

To assess the relative effects of these factors on skepticism, we estimated an ordinary least squares regression equation using the skepticism scale (table 2.2). Among whites, greater skepticism is strongly associated with being poor, uninsured, having no regular provider, and being in excellent, good, or fair health. Age, sex, and education also have significant effects on attitudes toward medical care. Among African Americans, age and health status are the only variables with a significant effect on skepticism, with older persons and those in poor health (the uncoded category) being the least doubtful. For Mexican Americans, those in excellent and good health are significantly more skeptical of medical care than those in poor health. Interestingly, neither poverty status, insurance coverage, nor provider status is related to skepticism among the two minority populations. Thus, for these groups, it appears that those in poor health, the group expected to have more contact with the system, are the least skeptical when all other factors are held constant. It should be noted that the variance explained is fairly low for all three groups, which suggests that many factors affecting skepticism are not included in the model.

Skepticism and Use of Health Services

Table 2.3 presents the bivariate relationships between skepticism and the three measures of use—blood pressure check, ambulatory contact, and mean number of ambulatory visits. For the total sample, 77 percent of whites, 80 percent of African Americans, and 63 percent of Mexican Americans had their blood pressure checked during the year prior to the survey (data not shown). The percentages having an ambulatory contact are 78, 70, and 64 percent for whites, African Americans, and Mexican Americans, respectively (data not shown). Among whites and African Americans, the likelihood of having a blood pressure check or an ambulatory contact in the last year is lowest for those high in skepticism. Among Mexican Americans, however, similar proportions of those with medium and high scores on skepticism report blood pressure checks in the past year, and both are less likely to do so than those low in skepticism. Mean number of visits also declines as skepticism increases among whites and African Americans. In contrast, among Mexican Americans, the bivariate results show a slight positive association between skepticism and mean visits, although the differences are not significant.

Table 2.4 presents the logistic regression analyses of the probability of having a blood pressure check in the last year. Among whites, those skeptical of medical care are less likely to have a blood pressure check. The probability of having blood pressure assessed is also related to being older, being more highly educated, being female, residing in a nonmetropolitan area, being uninsured, having no regular provider, being in poorer health, and being hypertensive. Being female, uninsured, having no regular provider, being skeptical, and being hypertensive also affect the probability that African Americans have their pressure checked, although health status is not a significant factor.

Findings for Mexican Americans are similar to those for African Americans. The exceptions are that skepticism has no effect for

Mexican Americans, and the probability of Mexican Americans having their blood pressure checked is lower for those with a nonprivate provider as well as for those with no regular provider. The findings regarding nonprivate providers and blood pressure check indicate that Dutton's (1978) argument regarding the barriers encountered in the public health-care delivery system may be especially relevant for Mexican Americans. Health status, surprisingly, does not have a significant effect for Mexican Americans. It is important to note that there are no significant differences between those with private and public insurance in any of the three racial/ethnic groups. Having any type of coverage appears to encourage preventive care at least to the degree indicated by this one measure. This finding is surprising, given that many physicians do not accept patients with Medicaid health insurance coverage due to the program's low reimbursement rates. One possible explanation for the lack of a significant difference between those with private and public coverage could be that the privately insured may experience inadequate coverage and high out-of-pocket costs that deter use. Also once Medicaid patients find a doctor who accepts Medcaid patients, they may use services similar to those with private coverage. Similar to other studies reporting multivariate logistical analyses, the explained variance is quite modest.

Ambulatory contact is an indicator of whether respondents accessed the system at any time during the past year. Table 2.5 shows that whites who are uninsured, who are older, who have no regular provider, and who are skeptical of medical care are less likely to have an ambulatory contact. The probability of a contact is also greater for females and those with higher educational attainment, and increases with declining health status.

Similar to whites, the probability of having a contact is lower for African Americans and Mexican Americans who are uninsured and for those who have no regular provider, while the probability of contact is higher for females and those in poorer health. Skepticism has no significant effect for either African Americans or Mexican Americans. Similar to the finding for blood pressure check, there are no significant differences in the probability of a contact for those with public and private insurance in any of the three racial/ethnic groups. It is interesting to note, however, that among African Americans the sign of the coefficient is positive for public insurance coverage, while the sign is negative for whites and Mexican Americans.

Table 2.6 presents the results of the analyses of mean number of ambulatory visits among those who gained access to the health-care delivery system. Whites who reside in nonmetropolitan areas, who are uninsured or have public insurance, who are skeptical of medical care, and who have no regular provider have fewer visits than their counterparts. Being female, highly educated, and in poorer health are associated with increased numbers of visits. Among African Americans, having no regular provider and being skeptical of medical care reduce the number of visits, while being in poorer health increases the number of visits. The effects of being uninsured or having public coverage do not differ significantly from the effects of being privately insured. These results, together with those from the analysis of ambulatory contact, suggest that being uninsured hinders access to the system for Africans Americans. However, once they are in, the problems posed by lack of insurance are somewhat tempered. Mexican Americans have fewer visits if they are uninsured and if they are without a regular source of care, while being female and being in poorer health is associated with a greater number of visits. In contrast to whites and African Americans, for Mexican Americans, having a nonprivate provider significantly reduces the number of visits. Similar to the analyses of blood pressure check and ambulatory contact, the explained variance is low but consistent with comparable studies.

CONCLUSIONS AND POLICY IMPLICATIONS

The findings from this research suggest that insurance status, the availability of a regular provider, and health status are influential determinants of health service use among whites, African Americans, and Mexican Americans. For all three racial/ethnic groups, the uninsured and those without a regular provider are less likely to have a blood pressure check or an ambulatory contact with any health-care provider even when self-rated health status, an indicator of need, is controlled. In addition, among whites and Mexican Americans, lacking health insurance and a regular provider both are associated with fewer ambulatory visits for those having at least one contact with the system. Having no regular provider reduces the number of visits for African Americans, but insurance status has no significant effect. It appears that being uninsured acts to deter African Americans from accessing the system, but once they are in, insurance status plays no major role in the number of visits.

Skepticism remains statistically significant in predicting all indicators of use among whites, but is predictive of none among Mexican Americans. It is also predictive of the probability of having a blood pressure check and the number of ambulatory visits among African Americans. The multivariate analyses of factors related to skepticism indicate that whites who are poor, uninsured, have no regular provider, and are in excellent to fair health have more negative attitudes toward medical care. Among the two minority populations, only high evaluations of health status are associated with more skepticism. There is little evidence for a shift to a consumerist attitude among the young and affluent as suggested by some researchers (Cockerham et al. 1986; Haug and Lavin 1981, 1983). While younger persons are more skeptical in this analysis, increased education (which is correlated with higher income) is associated with fewer doubts regarding the efficacy of medical care.

The causal mechanisms that generate negative evaluations of health care are not clear. Persons with few health problems may be more doubtful of the health system's efficacy because they have less need for services. Thus, individuals experiencing only minor, acute illnesses may be more likely to engage in self-care and to believe that illnesses can be avoided by taking precautions. Franks et al. (1993) also argue that skepticism may be a "self-protective reaction to the barriers to care imposed by not having insurance." In other words, persons who are uninsured may rationalize their vulnerability by discounting the value of coverage. This argument may be especially applicable to whites in this study, given that the persons most skeptical also tend to be uninsured and without a regular provider. Also future studies may find that persons now in good health may become less skeptical as they experience greater health problems, given that they are able to access appropriate care. While this study focused on skepticism, future research should address the relative contributions of other attitudes that may be relevant for services use.

The findings from this research suggest that policymakers must confront such issues as insurance coverage and the availability of a regular health-care provider. Extending coverage to the uninsured may not have the anticipated impact if providers are unavailable. It is well known that the geographical concentration of physicians and the shortage of primary care physicians remain serious problems in this country. This study found that in each of the racial/ethnic groups, the uninsured and those without a provider encounter more barriers to care. However, it is important to note that these problems are more severe for African Americans and Mexican Americans. The proportion uninsured and proportion without a regular provider is highest for Mexican Americans, followed by African Americans.

In contrast to whites and African Americans, among Mexican Americans, type of provider affects selected services among Mexican Americans. Specifically, Mexican Americans are less likely to get a blood pressure check and have fewer ambulatory visits if their regular source of care is a nonprivate rather than a private provider. One possible explanation for these findings is that the impersonal climate associated with treatment in the public sector, as discussed by Dutton (1978), may be even more problematical for those with language barriers. Thus, inability to communicate effectively may discourage use among Mexican Americans, especially if treatment is sought in outpatient departments, emergency rooms, and clinics. Further investigation is needed, however, given that having a private or nonprivate provider did not affect ambulatory contact. In the analyses presented here, few differences in use emerged between those with public versus private insurance. This finding is somewhat unusual given that many physicians refuse to treat Medicaid patients due to the low reimbursement levels of the program. Theoretically, this should make access more difficult for those with public insurance. It is possible that public insurance programs have improved so much they now afford recipients access on par with those covered under private insurance policies. On the other hand, it is possible that the lack of differences stems from a deterioration of coverage and access for those with private coverage rather than any changes in public insurance programs. Failure to find a difference may reflect rising out-of-pocket costs for those with private insurance coverage and, consequently, more restricted access. It is well known that cost-sharing is increasing for those with private coverage. Moreover, the Rand Health Insurance Experiment demonstrated that greater cost-sharing is associated with lower use. These findings indicate that those with private coverage may be facing increasing difficulties.

It is important to point out that the measures used in this research do not address the quality of services received. Although those with public insurance may have as many contacts with medical providers as do those with private insurance, there is no guarantee that the quality of treatment is similar. This is the case regardless of whether equitable use is a consequence of improving public programs or of private coverage becoming less adequate. The current emphasis in the policy-making arena is on the uninsured. However, the long-standing problems associated with public-funded health care should not be overlooked.

REFERENCES

Aday, L.A., R. Andersen, and G. Fleming. 1980. *Health Care in the U.S.: Equitable for Whom?* Beverly Hills, CA: Sage.

Aday, L.A., and R. Eichorn. 1972. *The Utilization of Health Services: Indices and Correlates.* DHEW pub. no. (HSM) 73-3003. Rockville, MD: National Center for Health Services Research and Development.

Aday, L.A., G. Fleming, and R. Andersen. 1984. *Access to Medical Care in the U.S.: Who Has It, Who Doesn't.* Chicago: Pluribus Press.

Andersen, R., A. Giachello, and L.A. Aday. 1986. Access of Hispanics to health care and cuts in services: A state-of-the-art overview. *Public Health Reports* 101:238-252.

Andersen, R., J. Lion, and O. Anderson. 1976. *Two Decades of Health Services: Social Trends in Use and Expenditure.* Cambridge, MA: Ballinger.

Becker, M.H., C.A. Nathanson, R.H. Dracchman, and J.P. Kirscht. 1977. Mothers' health beliefs and children's clinic visits: A prospective study. *Journal of Community Health* 3:125-135.

Benham, L., and A. Benham. 1975. Utilization of physician services across income groups, 1963-1970. In *Equity in Health Services*, edited by R. Andersen, J. Kravits, and O. Anderson, 97-104. Cambridge, MA: Ballinger.

Berkanovic, E., and L.G. Reeder. 1974. Can money buy the appropriate use of services? Some notes on the meaning of utilization data. *Journal of Health and Social Behavior* 15:93-109.

Berkanovic, E., and C. Telesky. 1985. Mexican-American, Black-American, and White-American differences in reporting illnesses, disability and physician visits for illnesses. *Social Science and Medicine* 20:567-577.

Berkanovic, E., C. Telesky, and S. Reeder. 1981. Structural and social psychological factors in the decision to seek medical care for symptoms. *Medical Care* 19:693-709.

Blendon, R., L. Aiden, H. Freeman, and C. Corey. 1989. Access to medical care for black and white Americans: A matter of continuing concern. *Journal of the American Medical Assocation* 261(2):278-281.

Cockerham, W., G. Kunz, G. Lueschen, and J. Spaeth. 1986. Social stratification and self-management of health. *Journal of Health and Social Behavior* 27:1-14.

Cornelius, L. 1993. Ethnic minorities and access to medical care: Where do they stand? *Journal of the Association for Academic Minority Physicians* 4:16-25.

Council on Scientific Affairs. 1991. Hispanic health in the United States. *Journal of the American Medical Association* 265:248-252.

Davis, J.A. 1971. *Elementary Survey Analysis.* Englewood Cliffs, NJ: Prentice Hall.

Dutton, D. 1978. Explaining the low use of health services by the poor: Costs, attitudes, or delivery system. *American Sociological Review* 43:348-368.

Employee Benefit Research Institute. 1994. *Sources of Health Insurance and Characteristics of the Uninsured: Analysis of the March 1993 Current Population Survey.* Washington, DC: Issue Brief No. 145.

Franks, P., C. Clancy, M. Gold, and P. Nutting. 1993. Health insurance and subjective health status: Data from the 1987 National Medical Expenditure Survey. *American Journal of Public Health* 83(9):1295-1299.

Hadley, J., E.P. Steinberg, and J. Feder. 1991. Comparison of uninsured and privately insured hospital patients: Conditions on admission, resource use, and outcome. *Journal of the American Medical Association* 265:374-379.

Haug, M., and B. Lavin. 1983. *Consumerism in Medicine.* Beverly Hills, CA: Sage.

Haug, M., and B. Lavin. 1981. Practitioner or patient—Who's in charge? *Journal of Health and Social Behavior* 22:212-229.

Hayward, R., M. Shapiro, H. Freeman, and C. Corey. 1988. Inequities in health services among insured Americans. *New England Journal of Medicine* 318:1507-1512.

Jackson, J. 1980. Urban black Americans. In *Ethnicity and Health Care,* edited by A. Harwood, 37-129. Cambridge, MA: Harvard University Press.

Kleinman, J., M. Gold, and D. Markuc. 1981. Use of ambulatory medical care by the poor: Another look at equity. *Medical Care* 19:1011-1029.

Langlie, J. 1977. Social networks, health, beliefs, and preventive health behavior. *Journal of Health and Social Behavior* 18:244-260.

Newacheck, P.W. 1988. Access to ambulatory care for poor persons. *Health Services Research* 23:401-419.

Nickens, H. 1991. The health status of minority populations in the United States. *Western Journal of Medicine* 155:27-32.

Rundall, T., and J.R.C. Wheeler. 1979. The effect of income on use of preventive care: An evaluation of alternative explanations. *Journal of Health and Social Behavior* 20:397-406.

Sharp, K., C.E. Ross, and W.C. Cockerham. 1983. Symptoms, beliefs, and use of physician services among the disadvantaged. *Journal of Health and Social Behavior* 24:255-263.

Stahl, S., and G. Gardner. 1976. A contradiction in the health care delivery system. *Sociological Quarterly* 17:121-129.

Suchman, E. 1965. Social patterns of illness and medical care. *Journal of Health and Social Behavior* 6:2-16.

Treviño, F., and A. Moss. 1984. *Health Indicators for Hispanic, Black and White Americans.* DHHS pub. no. 84-1576. Washington, DC: Government Printing Office.

Treviño, F., E. Moyer, B. Valdez, and C. Stroup-Benham. 1991. Health insurance coverage and utilization of health services by Mexican Americans, mainland Puerto Ricans, and Cuban Americans. *Journal of the American Medical Association* 265(2):233-237.

US Bureau of the Census. 1993. *Hispanic Americans Today.* Current Population Reports, P23-183. Washington, DC: Government Printing Office.

US Department of Health and Human Services (US DHHS). 1985. *Report of the Secretary's Task Force on Black and Minority Health: Volume 1.* Washington, DC: Government Printing Office.

Weissman, J.S., R. Stern, L.S. Fielding, and A.M. Epstein. 1991. Delayed access to health care: Risk factors, reasons, and consequences. *Annals of Internal Medicine* 114:325-331.

Wolinsky, F. 1982. Racial differences in illness behavior. *Journal of Community Health* 8:87-101.

Table 2.1

Skepticism by poverty status, insurance status, source of care, and health status for whites, African Americans, and Mexican Americans, 1987

	WHITES						AFRICAN AMERICANS						MEXICAN AMERICANS					
	Low (percent)	Med (percent)	High (percent)	N	χ^2	γ^A	Low (percent)	Med (percent)	High (percent)	N	χ^2	γ^A	Low (percent)	Med (percent)	High (percent)	N	χ^2	γ^A
POVERTY STATUS					33.19**	-.12					5.24	.05					3.72	.02
Poor	34.6	41.2	24.2	710			55.8	31.2	13.0	502			51.9	33.3	14.9	140		
Near-poor	35.7	46.9	17.4	1,388			52.2	34.3	13.6	685			45.1	41.5	13.4	236		
Nonpoor	40.3	45.9	13.8	7,676			50.2	35.8	14.0	1,642			43.7	38.5	17.8	431		
INSURANCE STATUS					54.45***	-.15					14.50**	-.10					4.41	-.05
Uninsured	32.1	43.1	24.9	1,267			51.9	33.1	15.0	564			43.8	37.8	18.4	277		
Public	42.3	42.4	15.3	623			58.6	28.5	12.9	480			52.6	34.4	13.1	74		
Private	40.2	46.3	13.5	7,881			50.0	36.7	13.4	1,785			46.3	39.4	14.4	454		
REGULAR PROVIDER					28.06***	-.11					3.84	-.07					7.72	-.10
None	35.5	46.3	18.2	1,992			50.1	33.2	16.7	792			39.8	43.3	17.0	266		
Nonprivate	35.1	50.1	14.7	677			51.9	35.8	12.3	418			53.1	31.4	15.5	52		
Private	40.2	46.3	13.5	7,105			52.9	34.5	12.5	1,682			49.4	35.6	15.0	489		

Continued on next page

47

Table 2.1 continued

	WHITES						AFRICAN AMERICANS						MEXICAN AMERICANS					
	Low (percent)	Med (percent)	High (percent)	N	χ^2	γ^A	Low (percent)	Med (percent)	High (percent)	N	χ^2	γ^A	Low (percent)	Med (percent)	High (percent)	N	χ^2	γ^A
SELF-RATING OF HEALTH					67.16***	.10					25.73***	.16					8.23	.42
Poor	59.5	33.8	6.6	276			67.4	25.3	7.3	141			71.3	24.8	3.9	31		
Fair	45.5	40.2	14.4	1,321			57.7	33.1	9.2	639			52.0	38.7	9.4	189		
Good	38.3	47.4	14.4	5,208			50.4	35.4	14.3	1,508			44.7	39.3	16.1	420		
Excellent	37.9	45.9	16.8	2,969			45.3	35.7	19.0	541			38.7	37.0	24.3	167		

SOURCE: 1987 National Medical Expenditure Survey

NOTE: Percents may not sum to 100 due to rounding.

A Gamma (γ) indicates the strength and direction of the relationship between the two variables and ranges from - 1.00 to +1.00.

**p < 0.01   ***p < 0.001

Table 2.2
Regression analyses of skepticism for whites, African Americans, and Mexican Americans

	WHITES	AFRICAN AMERICANS	MEXICAN AMERICANS
AGE A	-.02***	-.03*	-.02
GENDER			
Female	-.14*	.00	-.19
Male	Reference group	Reference group	Reference group
EDUCATION A	-.08***	-.02	-.06
POVERTY STATUS			
Poor	.63**	.17	-.97
Near-poor	.31	.08	-.47
Nonpoor	Reference group	Reference group	Reference group
LOCATION OF RESIDENCE			
Non-SMSA	.10	-.58	-.01
Small SMSA	.02	.03	.53
Largest SMSA	Reference group	Reference group	Reference group
INSURANCE			
Uninsured	.89***	.24	.85
Public insurance	-.01	-.27	.22
Privately insured	Reference group	Reference group	Reference group
REGULAR PROVIDER			
Nonprivate provider	.36	.16	-.14
No regular provider	.48***	.31	.74
Private provider	Reference group	Reference group	Reference group
SELF-RATING OF HEALTH			
Excellent health	2.56***	2.26***	3.06*
Good health	2.23***	1.86***	2.32*
Fair health	1.72***	1.00***	.92
Poor health	Reference group	Reference group	Reference group
CONSTANT	12.71	12.60	12.13
R^2	.03	.03	.07

SOURCE: 1987 National Medical Expenditure Survey
A Continuous variable
$*p < 0.05$ $**p < 0.01$ $***p < 0.001$

Table 2.3

Blood pressure check, ambulatory contact, and mean number of ambulatory visits by skepticism, 1987

	WHITES					AFRICAN AMERICANS					MEXICAN AMERICANS				
	Low	Med	High	χ^2	γ^A	Low	Med	High	χ^2	γ^A	Low	Med	High	χ^2	γ^A
BLOOD PRESSURE CHECKED				54.40***	-.13				9.48**	-.06				2.63	-.11
No (percent)	19.1	23.9	29.4			16.9	21.4	25.7			32.7	38.9	37.9		
Yes (percent)	80.9	76.1	70.6			83.1	78.6	74.3			67.3	61.1	62.1		
N	3,529	4,355	1,480			1,253	960	384			320	295	124		
AMBULATORY CONTACT				36.36***	-.12				9.12**	-.11				3.78	-.16
No (percent)	20.0	22.1	28.9			27.8	30.7	38.7			32.5	36.2	47.3		
Yes (percent)	80.0	77.0	71.0			72.1	69.3	61.3			67.5	63.8	52.7		
N	3,844	4,430	1,500			1,450	984	395			376	302	129		
MEAN VISITS															
Mean	5.2	4.9	4.5			4.9	4.4	3.8			3.8	3.9	4.0		

Continued on next page

Table 2.3 continued

	WHITES	AFRICAN AMERICANS	MEXICAN AMERICANS
SCHEFF TEST B			
Low—medium	.05	.05	NS C
Low—high	.01	.01	NS
Medium—high	.05	.05	NS

SOURCE: 1987 National Medical Expenditure Survey

NOTE: Percents may not sum to 100 due to rounding.

A Gamma (γ) indicates the strength and direction of the relationship between the two variables and ranges from -1.00 to +1.00.

B Test of significance for contrast between low, medium, and high skepticism.

C Not significant

**p < 0.01   ***p < 0.001

51

Table 2.4
Logistic regression analyses of blood pressure check in the last year for whites, African Americans, and Mexican Americans

	WHITES	AFRICAN AMERICANS	MEXICAN AMERICANS
AGE A	.01*	.01	.00
GENDER			
Female	.49***	.43***	.70***
Male	Reference group	Reference group	Reference group
EDUCATION A	.07***	.04	-.01
POVERTY STATUS			
Poor	-.05	-.15	-.05
Near-poor	.02	-.16	-.25
Nonpoor	Reference group	Reference group	Reference group
LOCATION OF RESIDENCE			
Non-SMSA	-.31***	-.13	-.05
Small SMSAs	-.02	-.00	.04
Largest SMSAs	Reference group	Reference group	Reference group
INSURANCE			
Uninsured	-.50***	-.42*	-.71***
Public insurance	.15	.24	-.38
Private insurance	Reference group	Reference group	Reference group
REGULAR PROVIDER			
No regular provider	-.85***	-.85***	-.96***
Nonprivate provider	-.04	-.18	-1.00***
Private provider	Reference group	Reference group	Reference group
SKEPTICISM	-.05***	-.04*	.01
HEALTH STATUS B	.20***	.07	.21
HYPERTENSIVE	.87***	.68***	1.00***
CONSTANT	.77	1.58	1.11
R^2	.09	.08	.15

SOURCE: 1987 National Medical Expenditure Survey
A Continuous variable   B Coded 1 for excellent, 2 for good, 3 for fair, and 4 for poor.
$*p < 0.05$ $***p < 0.001$

Table 2.5
Logistic regression analyses of ambulatory contact in the last year for whites,
African Americans, and Mexican Americans

	WHITES	AFRICAN AMERICANS	MEXICAN AMERICANS
AGE A	.01***	.00	-.00
GENDER			
Female	.73***	.63***	.85***
Male	Reference group	Reference group	Reference group
EDUCATION A	.08***	.02	-.02
Poor	.06	.11	.21
Near-poor	.03	-.16	-.12
Nonpoor	Reference group	Reference group	Reference group
LOCATION OF RESIDENCE			
Non-SMSA	-.04	-.24	-.14
Small SMSAs	.10	-.19	-.06
Largest SMSAs	Reference group	Reference group	Reference group
INSURANCE			
Uninsured	-.53***	-.58***	-.69**
Public insurance	-.11	.31	-.22
Private insurance	Reference group	Reference group	Reference group
REGULAR PROVIDER			
No regular provider	-.96***	-1.24***	-.93***
Nonprivate provider	-.17	-.22	-.10
Private provider	Reference group	Reference group	Reference group
SKEPTICISM	-.04***	-.02	-.05
HEALTH STATUS B	.37***	.47***	.33*
CONSTANT	.27	.64	2.14
R^2	.09	.16	.15

SOURCE: 1987 National Medical Expenditure Survey
A Continuous variable   B Coded 1 for excellent, 2 for good, 3 for fair, and 4 for poor
$*p < 0.05$ $**p < 0.01$ $***p < 0.001$

Table 2.6

Regression analyses of number of ambulatory visits among those with one or more visits for whites, African Americans, and Mexican Americans

	WHITES	AFRICAN AMERICANS	MEXICAN AMERICANS
AGE A	.01**	.03***	.00
GENDER			
Female	1.05***	.31	.64*
Male	Reference group	Reference group	Reference group
EDUCATION A	.12***	.04	.04
POVERTY STATUS			
Poor	.19	-.17	-.14
Near-poor	-.09	-.26	-.41
Nonpoor	Reference group	Reference group	Reference group
LOCATION OF RESIDENCE			
Non-SMSA	-.53***	-.22	-.14
Small SMSAs	-.13	-.27	-.02
Largest SMSAs	Reference group	Reference group	Reference group
INSURANCE			
Uninsured	-.62***	-.42	-.98**
Public insurance	-.75***	.31	-.49
Private insurance	Reference group	Reference group	
REGULAR PROVIDER			
No regular provider	-.78***	-.60*	-.92***
Nonprivate provider	-.23	.04	-.92**
Private provider	Reference group	Reference group	Reference group
SKEPTICISM	-.05***	-.06**	.01
HEALTH STATUS B	1.00***	1.10***	.88***
CONSTANT	2.54	1.79	2.67
R²	.10	.12	.11

SOURCE: 1987 National Medical Expenditure Survey
A Continuous variable
B Coded 1 for excellent, 2 for good, 3 for fair, and 4 for poor.
$*p < 0.05$ $**p < 0.01$ $***p < 0.001$

A Comparison of Health Care Expenditures, by Income Across Racial and Ethnic Groups

M. Edith Rasell and Jared Bernstein

The problem of high expenditures for health care is well known. In 1993, an estimated $900 billion was spent to purchase health care, nearly 14.5 percent of national income or gross domestic product. What is not well known is who bears the burden of these high expenditures. Federal and state governments, businesses, and insurance companies are major funding sources. However, these are just intermediate sources of payment. Ultimately, individuals and families pay health-care costs through out-of-pocket spending, premiums paid to insurance companies, and taxes to federal, state, and local governments. Even insurance premiums paid for by employers are, for the most part, offset by reductions in wages and salaries. Thus, high expenditures for health care, while constituting a large outlay for business and government, ultimately are borne by and have their greatest impact on the budgets of families and individuals.

This examination focuses on families' outlays for health care. Many analyses of individual or family health-care spending use expenditures as a measure of health services received. This is not the case here. Our concern is not to quantify services received but to determine the level of actual outlays for health care by families to learn how these vary by race/ethnicity and other socioeconomic and demographic factors.

This study analyzes statistically matched microdata to examine health-care spending for white and minority families, specifically African Americans and Hispanics. We find the following:

- Without controlling for any of the factors that influence health-care spending such as health status, age, or education, all types of health care spending are lower, on average, for African American and Hispanic families than for white families.

- However, African American families in the upper three-fifths of the income distribution spend more in absolute terms on premiums than do whites in the same income bracket. The same is true for Hispanics in the middle quintile. Minority families in the lower two quintiles spend less than whites on premiums.

- After controlling for many of the factors that determine health-care spending—income, health status, insurance status, age, family size, education, and region of the country—total health expenditures by minority families are less than those by white families. At the means of the variables, total expenditures by minority families with group health insurance are 6 percent less than by white families. However, spending for premiums by minority families is 2 percent ($44) greater than spending by white families.

- While families of all races and ethnicity covered by public insurance (primarily Medicaid in this sample of the nonelderly) or nongroup insurance or that are uninsured spend less than do families with group health insurance, minority families with public insurance spend less than white families with public insurance.

REVIEW OF THE LITERATURE

Only a few recent studies have examined the distribution of health expenditures among families at different income levels (Rasell and Tang 1994; Rasell, Bernstein, and Tang 1993; Zedlewski et al. 1993; Holahan and Zedlewski 1992). The work by Rasell, Bernstein, and Tang shows expenditures to be very regressively distributed, with low-income families paying twice the share of their income for health care as do high-income families. The distributions of out-of-pocket and premium expenditures are even more regressive. Purchases made through the tax system are progressive.

However, none of these analyses examines the distribution of costs among minority families or compares the relative levels of spending and the distributions for minorities and whites. The only such examination of which we are aware uses data from the 1977 National Medical Care Expenditure Survey (NMCES). It finds that health-care spending by average-income households with nonwhite members was $138 less than that by average-income, white-only households. Health status, income, health-care access indicators, age, education, employment status, and a variety of other demographic and socioeconomic variables were held constant (Cantor 1988, 224).

METHODOLOGY AND DATA

The data on health-care spending used in this study come from three main sources: the 1987 National Medical Expenditure Survey (NMES), the 1987 Consumer Expenditure Survey (CEX), and the March 1993 Supplement to the Current Population Survey (CPS). Public-sector health-care expenditures were taken from the Census Bureau's *State Government Finances* and from *Significant Features of Fiscal Federalism* by the Advisory Commission on Intergovernmental Relations.

The primary data set is the NMES, a household survey of a nationally representative sample of the civilian, noninstitutionalized population. (See Appendix.) A series of interviews provided information on the use of health services and expenditures. In the supplemental Health Insurance Plans Survey, employers, unions, and other groups and agents that provided health insurance to survey participants, as well as insurance companies, were surveyed for data on premium costs. Because no premium information was obtained on 38 percent of policyholders, we imputed premiums and the employer share of premiums for these records using both a regression model and a hot deck procedure. For details of the imputation procedure, see Rasell, Bernstein, and Tang (1993). Demographic and socioeconomic data also are from the NMES.

The NMES, however, contains no information on health care paid for by governments with revenues from income, sales, and excise taxes. Since the public sector accounts for over one-third of all health-care expenditures—primarily for the Medicaid, Medicare, and public health programs—its outlays should not be omitted. The incidence of payroll taxes, including the Medicare health insurance tax, was calculated from the NMES wage data. The CEX, a nationally representative survey of consumption of all types, is the source for sales and excise taxes. Using a weighted hot deck technique, consumer units in the CEX were statistically matched to families in the NMES with family income, age of family reference person, family size, urban/rural location, and census region serving as match variables.

Once the 1987 data were assembled, they were aged to 1992. The March 1993 CPS provided the target figures for demographic variables, health insurance status, and an initial income distribution. After reconfiguring CPS families to correspond to the family structure in the NMES, average NMES family incomes, by cell, were adjusted to equal average CPS family incomes in corresponding cells. Variables used to construct the cells included *age of family reference person* (four categories), *race* (two categories), *education* (five categories), and *earner* status (married with two earners; married with zero or one earner or male single-headed household; female single-headed household; single person). After total family income was aged to fit the CPS distribution, further adjustments to income components were made based on the National Income Accounts and administrative data.

Following the income aging, family weights were adjusted to give the poverty and health insurance coverage rates found in the CPS. Out-of-pocket health expenditures and premium payments were aged to meet totals published by the Health Care Financing Administration, with modifications based on the work of Cowan and McDonell (1993).

Income tax information was obtained from the 1993 March CPS. Marginal and effective federal personal income tax rates and state effective income tax rates were statistically matched to filing units in the NMES data using a weighted hot deck technique. Match variables included filing unit type (single, household head, joint), filing unit size, number of filing unit members age 65 or above, total income, percent of income from wage and salaries, and percent from public transfers. The distributions of income and tax liabilities were then checked against those developed by the Congressional Budget Office (CBO 1994), and incomes and taxes were modified to offset the topcoding in NMES and the March 1993 CPS. Although all these data are for 1992, to reflect more accurately the distributional outcome of health financing changes that might be enacted in the future, tax changes from the Omnibus Budget Reconciliation Act of 1993 have been incorporated into the data.

In 1992, $48 billion, or approximately 30 percent of all federal health-care spending not funded through earmarked taxes (e.g., payroll taxes for Medicare), was financed with deficit spending. This is the same as the relationship between deficit spending and nonearmarked revenues in the federal budget as a whole. In the model used in this chapter, the deficit is fully funded through a mix of personal income taxes (48%), payroll taxes (43%), and corporate taxes (10%)—the relative proportions of these three taxes in 1992 federal revenues.

Having determined tax liabilities for each family in the NMES sample and knowing the share of total tax revenues these liabilities comprise as well as the share of revenues expended for health care at each level of government, health-care expenditures can be allocated to all the NMES families through the tax system.

After constructing the matched data set, we determined total health-care expenditures, out-of-pocket purchases, and premiums for white, African American, and Hispanic families. The unit of analysis is the family, or single person in single-person households, and all expenditures are summed over the family. Although using families as the unit of analysis creates numerous problems, they are more manageable than the problems associated with a similar analysis of individuals. The latter would introduce autocorrelation into the multivariate analysis since members of the same family would likely have correlated error terms. In addition, since health insurance often provides coverage for people who are not policyholders, attributing premium costs also would have been difficult. Family tax payments also would have needed to be distributed among all members.

Family health insurance is defined as the type of insurance coverage held by either the family reference person or the spouse of the reference person if one was present during the fourth interview of the survey. When more than one type of insurance was identified, the family was assigned insurance according to a hierarchy of coverage: employer- or union-sponsored group insurance took precedence over public insurance (primarily Medicaid in this nonelderly sample), and the latter had precedence over nongroup insurance. Families were considered to be uninsured if neither the reference person nor spouse had any type of insurance.

The analysis estimates health-care expenditures as a share of family income for families in five different income groups (quintiles), with equal numbers of families—weighted with the sample weights—in each quintile. The 20 percent of families with the lowest incomes are in the first quintile, the 20 percent of families with the second lowest incomes are in the second quintile, and so forth, with the 20 percent of families with the highest incomes in the fifth quintile. Results are then reported by family modified economic income quintile. Family modified economic income is the sum of money income plus cash transfers, employer contributions for employee health insurance, the employer share of the federal payroll tax, corporate taxes, and employer contributions for unemployment insurance. Since portions of these components of economic income are used to purchase health care and thus are included in health-care spending, they must also be included in family income. The sample includes only families with reference persons less than age 65. The reference person, as identified in the NMES, is the person in whose name the residence is owned or rented.

Only white, African American, and Hispanic families are included in the analysis. Race/ethnicity of families is assigned based on the race/ethnicity of the family reference person.

DESCRIPTIVE ANALYSIS

The distribution and level of spending for health care, both in dollar amounts and as a share of income, was examined by quintile for white, African American, and Hispanic families and the combined sample of minority families.

For white families, the distribution of total health-care spending is regressive, with families in the lowest quintile spending a share of income that is 32.6 percent greater, on average, than families in the fifth and highest quintile. (Table 3.1.) Among African American and Hispanic families, those in the middle quintiles spend the largest share of income, and spending declines with both increases and decreases in income. Throughout the income distribution, minority families spend smaller shares of income for health care than do white families, but the differences shrink with rising income.[1]

In each of the three racial/ethnic groups, out-of-pocket expenditures are the most regressively distributed component of spending. On average, families in the first quintile spend the largest share of income out-of-pocket. Moreover, for low-income families, the largest component of health expenditures is out-of-pocket spending, which accounts for approximately half of all expenditures (i.e., $652 out of $1,410). For families in the top quintile, out-of-pocket spending is just 10 to 12 percent of health expenditures.

In each racial/ethnic group, spending on premiums is lowest in the extremes of the distribution and highest for families in the third or fourth quintile. Although in the lowest quintile African American and Hispanic families spend a smaller share of income on premiums than do whites, minority families in the third, fourth, and fifth quintiles, on average, spend more in absolute terms for premiums than do white families.

Multivariate Analysis

Multivariate analysis allows a comparison of spending by race/ ethnicity while controlling for a number of other factors that influ- ence expenditures. Three separate models estimate the log of total expenditures, log of out-of-pocket spending, and premiums, while holding constant income, health status, type of insurance, family size, age and education of reference person, and region. A dummy variable indicating whether the family reference person is a member of a minority population, African American or Hispanic, shows the effect of race/ethnicity on spending. (The African American and Hispanic samples were pooled since mean differences in African American and Hispanic family expenditures were generally insignifi- cant and because of concern about efficient estimation of interaction terms.) In addition, including an interaction term of minority status with income allows the relationship between rising income and health expenditures to be race/ethnicity-specific. Dummy variables are also used to capture interactions between minority status and three types of health insurance: public insurance, nongroup insur- ance, and no insurance (uninsured). Group insurance is the omitted category. The means of the variables are shown in table 3.2. The models are estimated with ordinary least squares, using SUDAAN software. To estimate correctly the standard errors of the coefficients, special procedures were used to take into account the sampling characteristics.

The model of expenditures for premiums has some serious limitations. The data on premiums in the NMES are the sum of expenditures for the entire year. However, in these models, insurance status is assigned based on responses to questions asked in the fourth quarter of the year about insurance coverage during the previous four months. For many people, insurance coverage is unstable and may change from quarter to quarter or month to month. For example, in a 28-month period between 1987 and 1989, 73.5 percent of the population was continuously covered with either private health insurance, Medicare, or Medicaid (Short 1992). However, the remaining 26.5 percent either had changes in coverage or was uninsured throughout the period. Thus, premium expenditures in the NMCES may be greater than zero even when a family is uninsured in the fourth quarter of the year and is recorded as uninsured in this analysis. This issue will be discussed in more detail below.

Total expenditures. Table 3.3 shows the results of estimating the model of the log of total health-care expenditures. Spending rises with age, family size, and fair or poor health status. Spending also rises with increasing income, although the increase for families in the first quintile is significantly lower than for families in the rest of the income distribution. The intercept for minority families is significantly lower than for white families. Minority-specific income elasticity, however, is higher than that of whites, though insignificant at the 0.05 level. At the means of the variables among families with group health insurance, minority families spend 6 percent less than do white families.

Among both white and minority families with public or nongroup insurance or that are uninsured, spending is significantly reduced. Coverage with public insurance reduces expenditures by 68 percent, while being uninsured lowers spending by 32 percent. In addition, minority families with public insurance spend less than do white families with public insurance.

Out-of-pocket spending. The model of out-of-pocket spending is shown in table 3.4. Out-of-pocket spending rises with income, and this increase is the same for both white and minority families, although spending is lower for minority families than for white families. Spending rises with increases in family size, education, and worsening health status. Out-of-pocket expenditures by families with public insurance are lower than those by families with group insurance, and spending by minority families with public insurance is lower than that by white families. The uninsured also spend less out of pocket than do families with group health insurance; however, there are no differences associated with race/ethnicity.

Premiums. The model of spending on insurance premiums is shown in table 3.5.[2] Expenditures rise with family size and poor or fair health status. There are significant regional differences. Compared to expenditures in the West, spending is higher in the East and Midwest and lower in the South. Expenditures fall with increases in education.

Spending on premiums rises with income, with a greater increase for families in the highest 20 percent of the income distribution.[3] Minority families have a higher intercept but a lower rate of increase than do whites. Among families with group health insurance, minority families spend 2 percent ($44) more than white families at the means of the variables. On average, families with public or nongroup insurance or that are uninsured (in the fourth quarter of the year) spend significantly less on premiums than do families with group insurance. Minority families that are uninsured or have public insurance spend significantly less on premiums than do white families.

DISCUSSION AND CONCLUSION

The examination of the raw data shows large spending differences between minority and white families. Even within income quintiles, minority families spend less than white families, both in actual dollars and as a share of income. Average total health-care spending, out-of-pocket expenditures, and spending on premiums all are lower for minority families than for white families. The finding that African American families in the upper three quintiles, and Hispanics in the third quintile, spend more on premiums in absolute terms than do whites needs to be confirmed and examined further.

When a range of factors that influence health-care spending, such as income, education, health status, age, family size, and region of residence, also are taken into account, a much more complex pattern is revealed. Families that have public health insurance or are uninsured (during the fourth quarter) spend less out-of-pocket than do families with group health insurance, irrespective of race/ethnicity. This may be because Medicaid benefits are quite broad, assuming that a participating physician can be found, and copayments and coinsurance are seldom required. These findings also suggest that the uninsured are not buying services directly out-of-pocket to compensate for their lack of insurance.

Uninsured minority families spend significantly less on premiums than do uninsured white families. It would be tempting to argue that this could, in part, be explained by differences associated with race/ethnicity in the length of uninsured spells, which is obscured by the limitations of our model, as described above. However, Swartz, Marcotte, and McBride (1993) show that race is not a significant factor in determining the length of uninsured spells, holding constant income, industry, employment status, education, age, and other factors. Moreover, among people with poverty-level incomes, race is not a significant determinant of whether a spell without insurance ends with private insurance coverage. Low-income members of both white and minority populations are equally likely to end an uninsured spell by acquiring private insurance and paying a premium. However, Swartz et al. also find that minority status significantly increases the likelihood that low-income individuals will end an uninsured spell with enrollment in Medicaid, a finding that could explain the lower out-of-pocket spending.

Among families with public health insurance, minority families also spend significantly less on premiums than do white families. This could be due to the relative lengths of time families are enrolled in Medicaid, a hypothesis we cannot test with this model. We raise this possibility because Medicaid coverage is often of short duration. Over a 28-month period in 1987-89, 10.8 percent of the population was enrolled in the Medicaid program at some point. However, 36 percent of beneficiaries were enrolled for one year or less (Short 1992). Moreover, it appears that the length of a spell of Medicaid coverage tends to be longer for minorities than for whites. Of all white individuals enrolled in Medicaid during the period, 40.5 percent were enrolled for 12 or fewer months, and 35 percent were enrolled for 28 or more months. Among black beneficiaries, 28.5 percent were enrolled for 12 or fewer months, and 50 percent were enrolled for 28 or more months (Short 1992). If white disenrollees were uninsured, this would not increase their premium expenditures. However, if they purchased either group or nongroup insurance, this would raise their spending on premiums compared to blacks who remained Medicaid beneficiaries.

Another interesting finding is that premium expenditures decline with rising education levels. Since education is positively correlated with health status and because most premiums are purchased through an employer, this may reflect a well-functioning system of experience rating among and within firms.

These findings indicate that socioeconomic and demographic characteristics other than race/ethnicity explain much of the difference in health-care spending between white and minority families. Thus, policies that target socioeconomic and demographic factors to address the causes of high expenditures would benefit African American and Hispanic families as well as white families. Measures to reduce out-of-pocket spending and place greater reliance on tax-based financing in place of premiums would lessen the health-cost burden for low- and middle-income families and likely improve access as well. These measures would also benefit those in relatively poorer health and slow the rise in spending that accompanies increases in age. Community rating, structured in ways so as not to drive the healthy out of the market, is also important.

N OTES

1. A series of *t*-tests showed that spending (both levels and shares) by white families was significantly higher than that by African American and Hispanic families. This result holds in every case for overall averages and in almost every case for quintile levels and shares. Differences between African American and Hispanic families, however, were generally insignificant, particularly among the quintiles. The *t*-tests between whites and minorities (African American and Hispanic families combined) were significant.

2. A Tobit model would probably have been preferred. However, the software required for analyzing the NMES data (SUDAAN) does not permit estimation of this functional form. Using a Tobit model to examine premium expenditures would be important in future work.

3. While we expect family spending on premiums to rise with income, we are suspicious of the magnitude of this result, which suggests that a 1 percent rise in income would lead to a $422 rise in premium spending (for wealthy families, the increase would be $474 at the margin). This represents a 20 percent rise in premium spending over the average value. It is likely that this result reflects omitted variable bias. While we attempted to control for job quality, which is positively correlated with both income and premiums, with a set of one-digit industry controls and establishment-size dummies, the fairly crude nature of the proxies may have failed to extract fully the job quality component from the income variable.

REFERENCES

Cantor, J.C. 1988. The burden of financing health care in the United States. Sc.D. Dissertation, Johns Hopkins University.

Congressional Budget Office (CBO). 1994. *An Economic Analysis of the Revenue Provisions of OBRA-93.* Washington, DC: Government Printing Office.

Cowan, C.A., and P.A. McDonell. 1993. Business, households, and Governments: Health spending, 1991. *Health Care Financing Review* 14(3):227-248.

Holahan, J., and S. Zedlewski. 1992. Who pays for health care in the United States? Implications for health care reform. *Inquiry* 29: 231-248.

Rasell, E., J. Bernstein, and K. Tang. 1993. *The Impact of Health Care Financing on Family Budgets.* Washington, DC: Economic Policy Institute.

Rasell, E., and K. Tang. 1994. *Paying for Health Care: Affordability and Equity in Proposals for Health Care Reform.* Washington, DC: Economic Policy Institute.

Short, K. 1992. *Health Insurance Coverage: 1987-1990 (Selected Data From the Survey of Income and Program Participation).* US Bureau of the Census, Current Population Reports, Series P-70, No. 29. Washington, DC: Government Printing Office.

Swartz, K., J. Marcotte, and T.D. McBride. 1993. Personal characteristics and spells without health insurance. *Inquiry* 30(1):64-76.

Zedlewski, S., J. Holahan, L. Blumberg, and C. Winterbottom. 1993. *The Distributional Effects of Alternative Health Care Financing Options.* Washington, DC: The Urban Institute.

Table 3.1
Average health care expenditures, and percent uninsured, by quintile and race/ethnicity, 1992

Quintiles	N	TOTAL EXPENDITURE[a]		OUT-OF-POCKET SPENDING		PREMIUMS		UNINSURED
		Level (dollars)	Share of Income (percent)	Level (dollars)	Share of Income (percent)	Level (dollars)	Share of Income (percent)	Percent of Families Uninsured
ALL								
Less than $15,848	1,772	1,410	17.7	652	9.4	315	3.4	37.1
$15,848–28,556	1,799	3,768	17.0	947	4.4	1,153	5.2	29.3
$28,557–43,770	1,805	5,976	16.6	1,045	2.9	1,973	5.5	16.2
$43,771–65,079	1,818	8,746	16.4	1,320	2.5	2,888	5.4	7.4
More than $65,079	1,751	16,766	14.9	1,686	1.8	3,547	3.8	6.1
Average	8,945	7,332	16.5	1,130	4.2	1,975	4.7	17.9
WHITE								
Less than $15,848	955	1,610	19.9	746	10.7	369	3.9	37.8
$15,848–28,556	1,101	3,980	17.8	1,066	4.9	1,182	5.2	27.2
$28,557–43,770	1,202	6,048	16.8	1,087	3.0	1,958	5.5	13.6
$43,771–65,079	1,315	8,829	16.5	1,376	2.6	2,883	5.4	5.5
More than $65,079	1,407	17,110	15.0	1,719	1.8	3,536	3.8	4.9
Average	5,980	8,135	17.0	1,239	4.2	2,129	4.8	14.1

Continued on next page

Table 3.1 continued

Quintiles	N	TOTAL EXPENDITURE[A]		OUT-OF-POCKET SPENDING		PREMIUMS		UNINSURED
		Level (dollars)	Share of Income (percent)	Level (dollars)	Share of Income (percent)	Level (dollars)	Share of Income (percent)	Percent of Families Uninsured
AFRICAN AMERICAN								
Less than $15,848	603	1,063	14.0	507	7.5	240	2.5	29.0
$15,848–28,556	466	3,317	15.2	636	3.0	1,176	5.4	25.7
$28,557–43,770	401	5,579	15.7	770	2.2	2,062	5.8	14.8
$43,771–65,079	332	8,302	15.7	947	1.8	3,113	5.9	14.6
More than $65,079	234	13,012	14.2	1,209	1.4	3,817	4.4	13.7
Average	2,036	4,335	14.8	700	4.2	1,460	4.4	23.6
HISPANIC								
Less than $15,848	214	1,090	13.8	467	6.8	196	2.2	49.4
$15,848–28,556	232	3,066	14.0	631	3.0	953	4.3	40.9
$28,557–43,770	202	5,825	16.5	1,028	2.9	1,997	5.7	37.2
$43,771–65,079	171	8,186	15.5	1,037	1.9	2,649	5.0	22.7
More than $65,079	110	13,310	14.1	1,537	1.7	3,425	3.9	26.0
Average	929	4,497	14.6	783	3.9	1,345	4.0	37.4

Table 3.1 continued

Quintiles	N	TOTAL EXPENDITURE[A] Level (dollars)	TOTAL EXPENDITURE[A] Share of Income (percent)	OUT-OF-POCKET SPENDING Level (dollars)	OUT-OF-POCKET SPENDING Share of Income (percent)	PREMIUMS Level (dollars)	PREMIUMS Share of Income (percent)	UNINSURED Percent of Families Uninsured
COMBINED AFRICAN AMERICAN AND HISPANIC								
Less than 15,848	817	1,073	13.9	492	7.3	224	2.4	36.7
$15,848–28,556	698	3,206	14.7	633	3.0	1,077	4.9	32.9
$28,557–43,770	603	5,680	16.0	876	2.5	2,035	5.8	25.1
$43,771–65,079	503	8,254	15.6	984	1.9	2,921	5.5	18.1
More than $65,079	344	13,133	14.2	1,342	1.5	3,659	4.2	16.9
Average	2,965	4,400	14.7	733	4.1	1,414	4.2	29.4

SOURCE: 1987 National Medical Expenditure Survey

A Includes out-of-pocket expenditures, premiums, and payments through the tax system.

Table 3.2

Variable means

VARIABLE	MEAN
Ln family money income *(dollars)*	10.23
Ln minority family money income *(dollars)*	9.80
Ln family modified economic income *(dollars)*	10.35
Ln minority family modified economic income *(dollars)*	9.90
Minority[A]	0.22
Age[A] *(years)*	40.19
Family size *(people)*	2.63
Health status (1 = at least one family member with fair, poor health)	0.23
East	0.20
Midwest	0.25
South	0.34
Education[A] *(years)*	12.69
Public health insurance	0.10
Non-group health insurance	0.06
Uninsured	0.16
Minority[A] x public health insurance	0.05
Minority[A] x non-group health insurance	0.01
Minority[A] x uninsured	0.05
Total health expenditure *(dollars)*	7,332.05
Total out-of-pocket *(dollars)*	1,129.90
Premiums *(dollars)*	1,975.10

SOURCE: 1987 National Medical Expenditure Survey
[A] Family reference person

Table 3.3
Estimates of model of total health care expenditures
Dependent variable: log total expenditures
(*t*-statistics)

INTERCEPT	-0.72**	REGION	
	(-2.81)	East	0.02
Ln INCOME A	0.85**		(1.13)
	(34.94)	Midwest	-0.01
QUINTILE 1 x Ln INCOME A	-0.02**		(-0.64)
		South	-0.00
	(-4.54)		(-0.20)
QUINTILE 5 x Ln INCOME A	-0.00	West	Reference group
	(-1.48)	EDUCATION B	0.01
			(1.90)
MINORITY B x Ln INCOME A	0.07		
	(1.87)	INSURANCE STATUS	
		Public health insurance	-1.14**
RACE/ETHNICITY			(-16.99)
Minority B	-0.75*	Nongroup health insurance	-0.07**
	(-1.97)		(-3.04)
Non-Minority	Reference group	Uninsured	-0.39**
AGE B	0.01*		(-13.72)
	(2.28)	Group health insurance	Reference group
Age x age	-0.00	MINORITY INSURANCE STATUS	
	(-1.34)	Minority B x public health insurance	-0.33**
FAMILY SIZE	0.03**		(-3.24)
	(5.21)	Minority B x nongroup	
HEALTH STATUS B		health insurance	-0.03
Fair or poor	0.10**		(-0.54)
	(5.17)	Minority B x uninsured	-0.11
Good or excellent	Reference group		(-1.92)
		Minority B x group health insurance	Reference group
		Adjusted R2	0.82

SOURCE: 1987 National Medical Expenditure Survey
A Family modified economic income   B Family reference person
*p < 0.05   **p < 0.01

72

Table 3.4

Estimates of model of health care expenditures
Dependent variable: log out-of-pocket expenditures
(*t*-statistics)

INTERCEPT	0.09	REGION (continued)	
	(0.18)	Midwest	-0.11
Ln INCOME A	0.29**		(-1.45)
	(6.25)	South	0.18*
QUINTILE 1 x Ln INCOME	C		(2.33)
		West	Reference group
QUINTILE 5 x Ln INCOME	C	EDUCATION B	0.09**
MINORITY B x Ln INCOME A	0.14		(8.90)
	(1.63)	INSURANCE STATUS	
RACE/ETHNICITY		Public health insurance	-1.55**
Minority B	-2.28*		(-9.45)
	(-2.52)	Nongroup health insurance	-0.07
Non-minority	Reference group		(-0.62)
AGE B	0.00	Uninsured	-0.58**
	(0.24)		(-4.96)
AGE x AGE	0.00	Group health insurance	Reference group
	(1.44)	MINORITY INSURANCE STATUS	
FAMILY SIZE	0.39**	Minority B x public health insurance	-0.50*
	(20.58)		(-2.02)
HEALTH STATUS B		Minority B x nongroup health insurance	-0.37
Fair or poor	0.63**		(-1.13)
	(9.97)	Minority B x uninsured	0.14
Good or excellent	Reference group		(0.70)
REGION		Minority B x group health insurance	Reference group
East	-0.09	Adjusted R2	0.28
	(-1.10)		

SOURCE: 1987 National Medical Expenditure Survey

A Family money income
B Family reference person
*p < 0.05   **p < 0.01

C Model was estimated without quintile/income variables.

Table 3.5
Estimates of model of health care expenditures
Dependent variable: premiums
(t-statistics)

INTERCEPT	-2163.91**	REGION	
	(-5.61)	East	172.82**
Ln INCOME A	421.61**		(3.30)
	(11.59)	Midwest	139.77**
QUINTILE 1 x Ln INCOME A	2.61		(2.75)
	(0.45)	South	-172.13**
QUINTILE 5 x Ln INCOME A	53.31**		(-3.87)
	(9.54)	West	Reference group
		EDUCATION B	-23.76**
MINORITY B x Ln INCOME A	-126.42**		(-3.77)
	(-2.90)	INSURANCE STATUS	
RACE/ETHNICITY		Public health insurance	-1524.20**
Minority B	1352.68**		(-21.51)
	(2.97)	Nongroup health insurance	-616.84**
Non-minority	Reference group		(-8.28)
AGE B	-15.40	Uninsured	-1525.17**
	(-1.52)		(-29.57)
AGE x AGE	0.35**	Group health insurance	Reference group
	(2.86)	MINORITY INSURANCE STATUS	
FAMILY SIZE	252.31**	Minority B x public health insurance	-392.14**
	(20.11)		(-4.01)
HEALTH STATUS B		Minority B x non-group health insurance	54.00
Fair or poor	118.10**		(0.31)
	(2.82)	Minority B x uninsured	-238.40**
Good or excellent	Reference group		(-2.82)
		Minority B x group health insurance	Reference group
		Adjusted R2	0.48

SOURCE: 1987 National Medical Expenditure Survey

NOTE: The model of expenditures for premiums included 11 industry dummy variables. All were significant and negative, except for entertainment/recreation, which was insignificant. Manufacturing was the omitted category. There were also 4 establishment-size dummy variables. Three of these were significant and positive: 26-100 employees, 101-500 employees, and 500+ employees. The omitted category was establishment size of 1 to 9 employees.

A Family modified economic income   B Family reference person

**$p < 0.01$

The Relationship of Health Perceptions, Physical and Mental Health, and Language Use to Usual Source of Care

Ruth E. Zambrana

Information is very limited on the social, cultural, and health factors that determine health services sought by Hispanics, especially by subgroup. With the exception of the Hispanic Health and Nutrition Examination Survey (HHANES) (1982-1984) and the 1987 National Medical Expenditure Survey (NMES) (US DHHS 1992), national and state databases have inadequate racial/ethnic identifiers to conduct meaningful analyses of Hispanic subpopulations. Most of the research has been descriptive and has focused on lack of access to care, with an emphasis on barriers such as lack of health insurance, bilingual and bicultural barriers, and geographic distance (Valdez et al. 1993; Giachello 1994). Few, if any studies, have used a multivariate model or examined intergroup differences among Hispanic subpopulations because of their small sample sizes (Amaro 1993).

Hispanics are a relatively young population group with defined social and economic disadvantage due to low levels of education, high environmental stressors, and language and cultural barriers (US DHHS 1991). Existing data suggest that Hispanics bear a disproportionate burden of illness, disability, and mortality as a result of access to poor quality services, lack of a usual source of care with established referral networks to specialty care, and cultural and financial barriers. As a result, there is a pattern of delay in seeking health-care services (Cornelius 1993; Council on Scientific Affairs 1991). Some investigators have suggested that cultural attitudes and beliefs contribute to delayed patterns of care-seeking and a disproportionate burden of illness, while others have found that socioeconomic status, knowledge of existing services, and institutional discrimination are more powerful predictors of appropriate use of services than are cultural attitudes (Congress and Lyons 1992; Adler et al. 1993; Molina, Zambrana, and Aquirre-Molina 1994; Williams 1990; Lillie-Blanton et al. 1993).

The role of cultural attitudes and perceptions has not been directly studied. Rather, most investigations have used acculturation as a measure of cultural attitudes. Acculturation has been measured as a set of variables on language preferences and proficiency and other demographics such as place of birth and educational level. However, acculturation measures neither provide us with an understanding of how a cultural group perceives health practices, nor measure health behaviors from a cultural perspective (Molina, Zambrana, and Aquirre-Molina 1994). Several relationships have been established among acculturation and perceived health status, delay in seeking care, lack of a usual source of care, and more traditional attitudes. These attitudinal dimensions have not been well defined and may represent the effects of low educational level on perceptions of the role of health care in their lives. It is also likely that many of these studies measure the effects of socioeconomic status on health outcome, that is, sociocultural barriers to access to health-care services.

For those studies that have established links between acculturation and other health-related variables, it is difficult to assess the independent effects of culture. Although acculturation has been linked to an increased burden of morbidity and mortality, the interaction of this variable (measured as English language proficiency) with other important variables, such as physical health, mental health, and health perceptions across Hispanic subgroups, has not been adequately explored. The NMES data provide a unique opportunity to examine the associations among these variables.

The purposes of this study are to describe and examine differences by Hispanic subgroup in sociodemographic characteristics, health perceptions, physical and mental health, language use, and social support, as well as to assess the independent effects of these variables on the dependent measure, having a usual source of care versus no usual source of care. This study was guided by the following research questions:

- Are there differences in health perceptions across Hispanic subgroups?

- Are there differences in physical and mental health across Hispanic subgroups?

- Are there differences in perceived social support across Hispanic subgroups?

- Do health perceptions, perceived social support, and physical and mental health vary by language use and Hispanic subgroup?

- Do sociodemographic characteristics, health perceptions, physical and mental health, and perceived social support predict having a usual source of care?

The expected relationships among the variables are: (1) Significant differences among subgroups on health perceptions, perceived social support, and physical and mental health variables; (2) a negative relationship between health perceptions and having a usual source of care; and (3) a positive relationship between physical and mental health.

DATA AND METHODS

The data used in this analysis are from the household component of the 1987 NMES and the supplement on medical care use, produced by the Agency for Health Care Policy and Research (see Appendix). NMES uses a national probability sample of the U.S. civilian non-institutionalized population. The total Hispanic sample is 3,981 adults. A subsample of adult Hispanics (N = 1,699), ages 18 to 64, who are identified as Puerto Rican (13.4%, N = 226), Mexican American (62.5%, N = 1,052) or other Hispanic (24.1%, N = 421) is used in the current analysis. Puerto Ricans include only those who resided on the United States mainland at time of interview. The "other Hispanic" category consists of individuals who self-identified as "other Spanish" and "Latin American." Geographically, almost 60 percent of other Spanish and 40 percent of Latin Americans were located in the West and South. The second largest area of concentration was the mid-Atlantic, with 14.5 percent of other Spanish and 25.3 percent of Latin Americans. Close to 17 percent of each group was located in the South Atlantic.

All instruments were in English only and were translated at time of interview for non-English speaking respondents. Excluded were respondents who had a current visit for a pregnancy, those 17 years of age or less, and those 65 years of age or older. Cubans were also excluded, due to small sample size (N = 160).

Independent Variables and Measures

The data reported here include information on social and demographic characteristics, language use variables, health perceptions, physical and mental health, social support, and medical care variables. Sociodemographic characteristics include age, education, gender, insurance (any private, government only, uninsured), income status (income and family size), and marital status.

A *language use* variable was created using three language items: (1) "Is English your native language?" (2) "Are you fluent in English?" (3) "If your native language is not English, is it Spanish or other?" Individuals who did not have English or Spanish as their native language were excluded from these analyses (N = 38, 2.2%). Those respondents who reported English as their native language, and no other language but English, were in Group 1 (native English speakers). Group 2 (fluent English) included respondents who reported Spanish as their native language, but were fluent in English. Those individuals who reported Spanish as their native language and were not fluent in English were in Group 3 (Spanish).

Health perceptions were measured using 15 items (exhibit 4.1). Ten of the items, previously used in another study, form a unidimensional scale to measure the respondent's attitudes toward the value of medical care and health insurance (Franks et al. 1993). Five additional items were included to assess perceptions of health status. The combined set of 15 items measures perceptions and attitudes on the value of health care and health status. (See exhibit 4.1 for list of items.) Tests of internal consistency (Cronbach α) yielded a reliability coefficient of .887 for the total sample. The range of the reliability coefficients by Hispanic subgroup was .877 to .904. Table 4.1 presents the results of the reliability tests (internal consistency measures) conducted on the four scales used for these analysis for the total sample and by Hispanic subgroup). All items were rated on a 5-point scale from 1 = strongly disagree to 5 = strongly agree. The scores ranged from 15 to 75, with higher scores indicating a more negative perception of the value of medical care and their own health status.

Physical status scale, consisting of 7 items, measured subjective physical limitations (Stewart, Hays, and Ware 1988). Respondents were asked if they experience limitations such as the following: "trouble climbing stairs," "trouble walking one block." The response option was yes = 1 and no = 2. The scores ranged from 7 to 14, with lower scores indicating greater physical limitations. The Cronbach α coefficient was .886 on the total sample ($N = 1,699$), with a range by Hispanic subgroup from .879 to .893. (Table 4.1)

Mental health status scale was composed of five items. Respondents were asked "How often in the past month, have you felt nervous, calm, down, happy, and very down." Each item was rated on a 6-point scale (1 = none of the time to 6 = all the time). The scores ranged from 6 to 30, with higher scores indicating higher mental distress. The reliability analyses yielded a Cronbach α coefficient of .881 for the total sample, with a range of .866 to .892 by Hispanic subgroup. (Table 4.1)

Social support scale, consisting of five items, measured friend contact and perceived social support in the past month. Items were rated on a 7-point scale (1 = every day to 7 = none). Lower scores represent higher levels of perceived social support. The Cronbach α coefficient for this scale was .777, with a range of .759 to .800 by Hispanic subgroup.

The *usual source of care* variable was derived using 4 items from the 1987 NMES medical care supplement, including: "Do you have a usual source of care?" (yes, no). "Do you usually see a particular doctor?" "If you usually see a particular doctor, is the doctor a general practitioner or a specialist?" "If a specialist, type of specialist seen?" Data were also obtained on mean number of provider visits in the last 12 months.

The dependent variable is *having a usual source of care* or *no usual source of care*. For these analyses, all respondents who reported a usual source of care, with or without a provider, were included in the *usual source of care* group (N = 1,150). All others were included in the "no usual source of care" group (N = 549).

Analytic Strategy

The analyses have three aims: (1) to develop a sociodemographic and use-of-medical-care profile for each Hispanic subgroup in the sample and to examine differences across groups using chi-square (χ^2) tests of significance; (2) to examine differences across subgroups on health perceptions, physical and mental health, and perceived social support using analyses of variance (ANOVA); and (3) to assess differences within and across groups by language use on major study variables.

For all analyses, age, income status, education, marital status, and language use were recoded. Age was recoded into three categories: 18-24, 25-44, and 45-64. Income status was recoded into three categories: poor, near-poor, and low-income = 1; middle-income = 2; and high-income = 3. Education was recoded into three categories: less than high school education, high school graduate, and any college. Marital status and language use were dichotomized for final multivariate analyses into married and not married, and Spanish only and English fluency. Insurance status was a three category variable—any private, government only, and uninsured. Employment status was a dichotomous variable, employed versus not employed. In addition, a correlation matrix was generated to assess the associations among scales. Lastly, a set of multivariate analyses, using logistic regression, was conducted to examine the associations of the independent measures to the dependent outcome, *having a usual source of care*.

All analyses were weighted to adjust for unequal probabilities of selection. Due to the complex survey design of the NMES, the statistical package SUDAAN was used to obtain weighted parameter estimates and standard errors for the multivariate analyses.

Data Limitations

These data have limitations that need to be taken into account in interpreting the results. First, no indicators were used for severity of illness or present chronic condition. Therefore, we were unable to assess the influence of these measures on the medical care variables and other factors. Second, these data apply only to persons ages 18-64 in the three Hispanic subgroups under study. Past evidence suggests that Cubans, who were excluded because of small sample size, have different patterns of health status and outcomes from other Hispanic subgroups (US DHHS 1991).

RESULTS

Table 4.2 presents the social, demographic, insurance, and language-use variables for the three Hispanic subgroups. There are no significant differences for age and gender by Hispanic subgroup. However, there are significant differences by subgroup for level of education and poverty, marital, employment, and insurance status. Overall, other Hispanics are significantly more likely than Mexican Americans or Puerto Ricans to have some college education, to be employed, to have private health insurance, and to be native speakers of English. Mexican Americans are almost twice as likely as other Hispanics and more than twice as likely as Puerto Ricans to be uninsured. Puerto Ricans are more likely to have government insurance, but less likely to be married than the other two groups.

In examining language groups, approximately 39 percent of the total sample reported being native English speakers, 41 percent reported being native Spanish speakers but fluent in English, and approximately 20 percent were native Spanish speakers, not fluent in English. The three ethnic subgroups did not vary substantially in the percentage not fluent in English, with 21 percent of Puerto Ricans, 20 percent of Mexican Americans, and 19 percent of other Hispanics reporting that they were native Spanish speakers and not fluent in English.

Table 4.3 depicts the mean scores and confidence intervals of scales measuring the health perceptions, physical and mental health, social support, and self-rated health for the total sample and the Hispanic subgroups. The data reveal no significant differences in mean scores by subgroup on the health perceptions, social support, and self-rated health scales. Although the average scores on self-rated health did not differ, a larger percentage of Puerto Ricans (7.9%) than Mexican Americans (2.6%) or other Hispanics (4.4%) reported poor health status (data not shown). Physical health mean scores, however, were significantly lower for the Puerto Rican group, revealing greater limitations, compared to Mexican Americans and other Hispanics [$F(1,696) = 4.77$, $p < .01$]. The mean scores of the mental health status scale reveal significantly higher mental distress for Puerto Ricans compared to the other two groups [$F(1,696) = 2.93$, $p < .05$].

Correlational analyses were conducted to assess the association among mean scale scores by Hispanic subgroup on major independent variables. The patterns of correlations were similar for all three groups. Significant associations were noted between the following variables for the total sample: a negative correlation is revealed between mental and physical health ($r = -.364$, $p \leq .001$); and a positive correlation between health perceptions and physical health ($r = .336$, $p < .001$). Individuals with greater physical limitations experienced higher mental distress and reported less value for medical care.

Table 4.4 presents the mean scale scores of major independent variables by three language-use groups for the total sample and by Hispanic subgroup. Tests of significance were conducted using ANOVA with levels of significance for two-tailed tests of .05 or greater to assess differences on major study variables by language use. For the total sample, there were significant differences in health perceptions and physical health by language use. The Spanish-only group reported greater physical limitations and more positive perceptions of their health and of medical care than the English-only and fluent English/native Spanish group. There were no significant differences by language group within Hispanic subgroups on mean health perception and mental health scores. However, within groups, the mean physical health score for the Puerto Rican and Mexican-American Spanish-only groups reveal significantly greater physical limitations than the other two language groups. Further, the higher social support mean score of the Puerto Rican Spanish-only group (18.96) shows that this group perceives significantly less social support than the other Puerto Rican language groups [$F(220) = 4.59$, $p < .01$]. For other Hispanic groups, there were no significant differences by language use on any of the scales.

Table 4.5 shows the distribution of usual-source-of-care variables for the total sample and for each subgroup. For the total sample, about 65 percent reported having a usual source of care, while 35 percent reported no usual source of care. Among those respondents who reported having a usual source of care, approximately 41 percent reported seeing a physician, and close to 60 percent reported that they do not have a regular physician or that their physician is unknown. Interestingly, more than one-third of Mexican American and other Hispanic respondents report their usual source of care as a clinic, while only about one-quarter of the Puerto Rican respondents do so. There were no significant differences across groups on the usual-source-of-care variables.

Table 4.6 displays the parameter estimates for the independent variables used in the logistic regression analyses. Five independent variables were included in Model 1: health perceptions, social support, physical health, mental health status, and language use. The four scales were entered into the model as continuous variables. The language-use variable was recoded into English fluency versus not fluent in English. The dependent measure was coded as 1 = having a usual source of care. In Model 1, the only significant predictor of having a usual source of care was health perceptions (β = -0.04; $p \leq .001$). The results indicate that those individuals who were the least negative about their health and the value of medical care were the most likely to have a usual source of care.

A second model was run that included five additional independent variables: three Hispanic-origin groups using Mexican Americans as the reference group; trichotomous education variable (less than high school, high school completed, and any college); gender (male as the reference group); three age categories (18-24, 25-44, and 45-64, with 45-64 as the reference group); and a dichotomous employment variable using "not employed" as the reference group. Model 2 shows the results of the final adjusted logistic regression model. The significant factors associated with having a usual source of care were health perceptions (β = -.03, $p \leq .01$) and gender (β = -.60, $p \leq .001$). Consistent with the first model, health perceptions were inversely related to the likelihood of having a usual source of care. The unexpected finding, however, was that women were less likely than men to have a usual source of care. Having less than a high school education was negatively and significantly associated with having a usual source of care (β = -.32, $p \leq .10$).

DISCUSSION

This study sought to examine intergroup differences among Hispanics on sociodemographic characteristics, health perceptions, physical and mental health, perceived social support, and language use, as well as to assess the influence of these variables on having a usual source of care. The data reveal a distinct, yet not surprising, sociodemographic profile of the Puerto Rican group. Puerto Ricans are less likely to be employed, more likely to have public insurance, and less likely to be married than the other two groups. The profile of Mexican Americans shows that they are the least likely to be insured and report the smallest mean number of physician visits. These data suggest that Mexican Americans are the subgroup most at risk for unmet health-care needs. Future research needs to acknowledge these different patterns of care by Hispanic subgroup and to examine the relationship between these patterns and early prevention, screening, and detection of disease and illness, and quality-of-care issues.

The study proposed a set of expected findings regarding Hispanic subgroup differences on central study variables. The findings reveal significant differences on mental and physical health by Hispanic subgroup (table 4.3.) There were no differences on perceived social support and health perceptions across subgroups. Not unexpectedly, the Puerto Rican group reported greater physical limitations and mental health distress. These data confirm a set of at-risk physical, social, and psychological characteristics that have been demonstrated in prior national profiles (US DHHS 1991). The pattern of risk factors for this group may be related to lifestyle behaviors. It has been observed that Puerto Ricans have higher rates of alcohol and drug use for both men and women than do the other two Hispanic subgroups, which may contribute to greater physical limitations (US DHHS 1991). On the other hand, Mexican-American groups have been found to engage in more favorable lifestyle behaviors. These differences in behavioral risk factors may partly explain the higher scores on physical limitations among Puerto Ricans, in spite of the fact that Mexican Americans have more limited access to health care. Further, structural factors such as the high unemployment rates among Puerto Rican women in the Northeast, coupled with the greater incidence of single-female heads of household relative to other Hispanic groups, may also contribute significantly to higher mental distress, which influences perceived physical limitations. Since Puerto Ricans represent a racially mixed group, the effects of racial discrimination and the quality of health-care services in regions where Puerto Ricans are concentrated also may account for higher reported physical and mental health limitations (Williams 1990).

The results on language use reveal that individuals who are monolingual Spanish speakers of Puerto Rican and Mexican-American origin report greater physical limitations. Lack of proficiency in English is associated with lack of health insurance, lower levels of education, and multiple barriers in access to appropriate services. It is not surprising that individuals who lack proficiency in English may have less favorable health status due to less knowledge about existing health-care services and how to negotiate the health-care system. The link of Spanish-language use to higher functional limitations requires systematic investigation in future studies.

Individuals with the least negative perceptions of their health and the value of medical care were the most likely to have a usual source of health care. Overall health perception scores reveal that Hispanics value medical care. However, as has been demonstrated in several studies, Hispanics are the least likely to have a usual source of care due to financial, sociocultural, and institutional barriers. Equally important, close to 50 percent of the Puerto Rican and Mexican American groups have less than a high school education. Lower educational levels result in Hispanics having jobs that do not usually have health insurance benefits for an individual or a family. Lack of health insurance is strongly associated with lack of a usual source of care. These data suggest that perception of the value of medical care is perhaps not the sole determinant of usual source of care, but that institutional barriers may play a central role in determining access to a usual source of care.

Gender also was associated with having a usual source of care. The finding that females were less likely than males to have a usual source of care may be partly explained by the probable status of a number of females in the sample as recent immigrants. It is also conceivable that a number of the women had partners/husbands who were employed in positions that did not offer family health insurance and thus left the women without the financial means to seek regular care. A limitation of these analyses is that the female sample was not analyzed separately to assess single-household status and insurance status. Future studies need to examine the socio-demographic context of Hispanic women to determine their unique profile.

CONCLUSIONS AND IMPLICATIONS FOR FUTURE RESEARCH

These data identify distinct social, psychological, and health profiles of Hispanic subgroups. Differences in physical health and psycho-logical distress represent important predictors of health outcomes for Hispanic subgroups. These factors are highly related to quality-of-life conditions and institutional forms of discrimination. There is a need to investigate further the factors that contribute to physical limita-tions among the Hispanic population, especially women and Hispan-ics not fluent in English. The Puerto Rican profile suggests that they are at particularly high risk compared to other Hispanic groups; yet studies on this group are limited. In fact, the current HHANES has excluded Puerto Ricans, which certainly raises serious concerns about monitoring the health status of this group.

Future studies need to incorporate a more comprehensive set of variables, such as those used in this study, to help account for differences in health outcomes by Hispanic subgroup and by gender. To examine the role of culture and its effects on access to a usual source of care systematically, cultural beliefs regarding medical and health care and perceptions of health care institutions and providers must be measured. Socioeconomic effects and language use must be measured separately to account for the independent effects of these variables on having a usual source of care. Emphasis on a more comprehensive set of variables that influence medical effectiveness and patient outcomes can be useful in understanding the multiple factors that contribute to the differential health status of Hispanic subgroups in the United States (Zambrana, Kelly, and Raskin 1994).

REFERENCES

Adler, N.E., W.T. Boyce, M.A. Chesney, S. Folkman, and L. Syme. 1993. Socioeconomic inequalities in health. *Journal of the American Medical Association.* 269(24):3140-3145.

Amaro, H. Using national health data systems to inform Hispanic women's health. Paper presented at the National Center for Health Statistics Public Health Conference on Records and Statistics, July 19-21, 1993, Washington, DC.

Congress, E.P., and B.P. Lyons. 1992. Cultural differences in health beliefs: Implications for social work practice in health settings. *Social Work in Health Care.* 7(3):81-96.

Cornelius, L. 1993. Ethnic minorities and access to medical care: Where do we stand? *Journal of the Association of Academic Minority Physicians.* 4(1):16-25.

Council on Scientific Affairs. 1991. Hispanic health in the United States. *Journal of the American Medical Association* 265(2):248-252.

Franks, P., C.M. Clancy, M.R. Gold, and P.A. Nutting. 1993. Health insurance and subjective health status: Data from the 1987 National Medical Expenditure Survey. *American Journal of Public Health* 83(9):1295-1299.

Giachello, A.L. 1994. Issues of access and use. In *Latino Health in the U.S.: A Growing Challenge*, edited by C. Molina and M. Aquirre-Molina, 83-111. Washington, DC: American Public Health Association.

Lillie-Blanton, M., R.M. Martinez, A.K. Taylor, and B.G. Robinson. 1993. Latina and African American women: Continuing disparities in health. *International Journal of Health Services* 23(3):555-584.

Molina, C., R.E. Zambrana, and M. Aquirre-Molina. 1994. The influence of culture, class and environment on health care. In *Latino Health in the US: A Growing Challenge*, edited by C. Molina and M. Aquirre-Molina, 23-44. Washington, DC: American Public Health Association.

Stewart, A.L., R.D. Hays, and J.E. Ware, Jr. 1988. The MOS short-form general health survey: Reliability and validity in a patient population. *Medical Care* 26:724-735.

US Department of Health and Human Services (US DHHS), Public Health Service. 1992. *Improving Minority Health Statistics.* Washington, DC: Government Printing Office.

US Department of Health and Human Services (US DHHS), Public Health Service. 1991. *Health Status of Minorities and Low-income Groups*, 3rd ed. Washington, DC: Government Printing Office.

Valdez, R.B., A. Giachello, and H.R. Trias, P. Gomez, C. De La Rocha. 1993. Improving access to health care in Latino communities. *Public Health Reports* 108(5):534-539.

Williams, D.R. 1990. Socioeconomic differentials in health. *Social Psychology Quarterly* 53(2):81-99.

Zambrana, R.E., M. Kelly, and I. Raskin. 1994. *Patient Outcomes and Medical Effectiveness Research: An Annotated Bibliography Related to Race, Ethnicity and Clinical Condition.* AHCPR pub. no. 94-0076. Rockville, MD: US Department of Health and Human Services.

Exhibit 4.1

Health perception items

I'm healthy enough that I really don't need health insurance.

Health insurance is not worth the cost.

I'm more likely to take risks than the average person.

I can overcome most illnesses without help from a medically trained professional.

Home remedies are often better than drugs prescribed by a doctor.

My own behavior determines recovery.

I know my own health better than the doctor.

Luck is a big part of recovery.

Doctors only recommend necessary surgery.

Medical care is easily available without cash.

I feel bad lately.

I feel somewhat ill.

I resist illness well.

I am as healthy as anyone.

I am in excellent health.

Table 4.1

Cronbach α coefficients of scales for total sample and Hispanic subgroups

	TOTAL	MEXICAN AMERICANS	PUERTO RICANS	OTHER HISPANICS
	$N=1,699$	$N=421$	$N=1,052$	$N=226$
Health perceptions	.887	.890	.877	.904
Physical health	.886	.879	.891	.893
Mental health	.881	.879	.866	.892
Social support	.777	.772	.759	.800

SOURCE: 1987 National Medical Expenditure Survey

Table 4.2
Distribution of sociodemographic characteristics of Hispanic subgroups, 1987
(In percents)

	χ^2	TOTAL	MEXICAN AMERICANS	PUERTO RICANS	OTHER HISPANICS
		$N=1,699$	$N=1,052$	$N=226$	$N=421$
GENDER					
Female	NSA	50.02	50.79	46.05	50.25
Male		49.98	49.21	53.95	49.75
AGE IN YEARS	NSA				
18–24		21.84	23.18	22.12	18.22
25–44		55.46	55.91	52.66	55.38
45–64		22.70	20.92	25.22	25.91
INCOME STATUS	10.34*				
Low income		48.68	53.92	43.26	38.06
Middle income		32.39	31.57	30.59	35.52
High income		18.93	14.50	26.15	26.41
EDUCATION LEVEL	13.46**				
Less than high school		46.75	50.97	48.52	34.79
High school completed		27.69	27.61	28.90	27.23
Any college		25.56	21.42	22.58	37.98
EMPLOYMENT	11.34*				
Employed		69.39	69.87	58.22	74.38
Not employed		30.31	29.79	41.49	25.44
INSURANCE STATUS	21.82*				
Private		52.57	48.49	52.47	63.23
Public		13.10	9.64	28.91	13.25
Uninsured		34.04	41.52	18.33	23.35

Continued on next page

Table 4.2 continued

	χ^2	TOTAL	MEXICAN AMERICANS	PUERTO RICANS	OTHER HISPANICS
		N=1,699	*N*=1,052	*N*=226	*N*=421
MARITAL STATUS	7.03*				
Currently married		66.23	66.39	55.65	71.79
Other		33.77	33.46	44.35	28.21
LANGUAGE USE	14.70**				
Native English speaker		38.88	39.92	25.47	44.12
Native Spanish, but fluent in English		40.86	39.79	53.07	36.40
Native Spanish speaker		20.26	20.29	21.46	19.48

SOURCE: 1987 National Medical Expenditure Survey
NOTE: Percents may not sum to 100 due to rounding.
A Not significant
*$p < 0.05$ **$p < 0.01$

Table 4.3

Mean scores and confidence intervals on study scales by Hispanic subgroup
(In percents)

	TOTAL	MEXICAN AMERICANS	PUERTO RICANS	OTHER HISPANICS
Health perceptions	39.08	39.13	39.04	38.98
	(38.57,39.59)	(38.50,39.76)	(38.02,40.06)	(37.96,40.00)
Physical health	13.24	13.29	12.90	13.29
F(1,696)=4.77**	(13.14,13.34)	(13.15,13.43)	(12.47,13.33)	(13.09,13.49)
Mental health	11.47	11.27	12.18	11.62
F(1,696)=2.93*	(11.18,11.76)	(10.92,11.62)	(11.32,13.04)	(11.11,12.13)
Social support	18.34	18.31	18.71	18.22
	(17.99,18.69)	(17.92,18.70)	(17.65,19.77)	(17.67,18.77)
Subjective self-rating	2.02	2.03	2.08	1.95
health scale	(1.96,2.08)	(1.97,2.09)	(1.88,2.28)	(1.85,2.05)

SOURCE: 1987 National Medical Expenditure Survey
$*p < 0.05$ $**p < 0.01$

Table 4.4
Mean scores of variables by language use, 1987
(In percents)

	HEALTH PERCEPTIONS	PHYSICAL HEALTH	MENTAL HEALTH	SOCIAL SUPPORT
TOTAL (N=1,699)				
Native English speaker	35.39	13.39	10.46	16.25
Native Spanish, but fluent in English	35.52	13.18	10.34	16.68
Native Spanish speaker	33.34	12.70	10.14	16.43
	F(1,658)=3.65*	F(1,658)=15.95***		
PUERTO RICANS (N=223)				
Native English speaker	36.08	13.45	10.85	15.28
Native Spanish, but fluent in English	36.38	13.10	11.27	17.79
Native Spanish speaker	32.04	11.26	11.78	18.96
		F(220)=17.99***		F(220)=4.59**
MEXICAN AMERICANS (N=1,052)				
Native English speaker	35.01	13.42	10.38	16.41
Native Spanish, but fluent in English	35.86	13.23	10.20	16.46
Native Spanish speaker	34.05	12.84	9.98	16.35
		F(1,035)=7.84***		
OTHER HISPANICS (N=421)				
Native English speaker	36.03	13.30	10.51	16.22
Native Spanish, but fluent in English	33.81	13.09	9.96	16.41
Native Spanish speaker	32.31	13.15	9.59	15.18

SOURCE: 1987 National Medical Expenditure Survey
*$p < 0.05$ **$p < 0.01$ ***$p < 0.001$

Table 4.5
Usual source of care variables by Hispanic subgroup, 1987

	TOTAL	MEXICAN AMERICANS	PUERTO RICANS	OTHER HISPANICS
	N=1,699	N=1,052	N=226	N=421
HAVE USUAL SOURCE OF CARE *(percent)*				
(Yes responses)	65.34	63.44	74.34	65.27
USUAL SOURCE OF CARE *(percent)*				
Regular physician	41.20	41.76	37.18	41.90
Without regular physician	19.44	17.78	28.75	18.76
Unknown	39.36	40.46	34.02	39.34
PLACE OF USUAL SOURCE OF CARE *(percent)*				
Office	65.34	63.44	74.34	65.27
Clinic	34.66	36.56	25.66	34.73
TYPE OF USUAL DOCTOR *(percent)*				
General practitioner	32.09	34.62	27.87	27.89
Specialist	12.21	9.95	14.14	17.03
Unknown	55.69	55.44	57.99	55.08
MEAN NUMBER OF PROVIDER VISITS	3.58 (3.19,3.97)	3.01 (2.58,3.44)	4.44 (3.19,5.69)	4.58 (3.54,5.62)

SOURCE: 1987 National Medical Expenditure Survey
NOTE: Percents may not sum to 100 due to rounding.

Table 4.6
Parameter estimates of predictors of having a usual source of care
(N=1,699)

	MODEL 1	MODEL 2
INTERCEPT	3.03	3.26
HEALTH PERCEPTIONS	-0.04***	-0.03**
SOCIAL SUPPORT	-0.01	-0.00
PHYSICAL HEALTH	-0.08	-0.05
MENTAL HEALTH	0.03	0.02
LANGUAGE USE		
Fluent in English	0.05	-0.00
Not fluent in English	Reference group	Reference group
HISPANIC ORIGIN		
Puerto Rican		0.34
Other Hispanic		0.00
Mexican American		Reference group
EDUCATION		
Less than high school		-0.32*
High school graduate		-0.10
Any college		Reference group
GENDER		
Female		-0.60***
Male		Reference group
AGE		
18–24		-0.31
25–44		-0.29
45–64		Reference group
EMPLOYMENT STATUS		
Employed		-0.11
Not Employed		Reference group
Model χ^2	15.42***	7.81***

SOURCE: 1987 National Medical Expenditure Survey
*$p < 0.10$ **$p < 0.01$ ***$p < 0.001$

PART II

IMPROVING TIMELY AND APPROPRIATE USE OF HEALTH SERVICES

CHAPTER 5

What Accounts for the Dependency of African Americans and Hispanics on Hospital-Based Outpatient Care?

Llewellyn J. Cornelius and Zulema E. Suarez

Health care has become increasingly less accessible for all Americans. Alarm over the growing number of uninsured persons and burgeoning health-care costs underlie federal and state discussions and initiatives related to health-care reform. While accessibility of health care is a new concern for most whites, ethnic minorities such as Hispanics and African Americans have traditionally encountered barriers in the use of health services.

Despite vast cultural differences, Hispanics and African Americans in this country face similar access problems (Cornelius 1993a, 1993b; Cornelius, Beauregard, and Cohen 1991; Blendon et al. 1989). Members of both groups are more likely to be uninsured than the population as a whole and are more likely than whites to be without a usual source of care (Cornelius, Beauregard, and Cohen 1991; Short, Cornelius, and Goldstone 1990).

Further, Hispanics and African Americans consistently have been more dependent than whites on hospital outpatient departments (OPDs) and emergency rooms (ERs) for their care, settings that provide less continuity of care for their patients than physicians' offices or clinics (Fleming and Andersen 1986). According to one study, while only 4.4 percent of whites had a hospital clinic or an ER as their usual source of care, 15.5 percent of African Americans and 9.9 percent of Hispanics were regular users of these settings (Cornelius, Beauregard, and Cohen 1991). A study of a sample of

Hispanics living in Chicago found that 27 percent had a public regular source of care (Suarez 1988).

Despite these barriers, studies have found that the numbers of physician visits and hospital days for African Americans and Hispanics are comparable to those for whites (Andersen et al. 1987; Aday, Fleming, and Andersen 1984). Some contend that these and other similar findings reflect equity in the use of health services (Yelin, Kramer, and Epstein 1983; Link, Long, and Settle 1982). Other researchers interpret these findings to mean that the access problems for Hispanics and African Americans lie less in entry to the system and more in satisfaction with services and reported difficulty in obtaining care (Aday, Fleming, and Andersen 1984).

Dissatisfaction by Hispanics and African Americans with health-care services may be due to underlying differences in the organization and delivery of services in OPDs. Regular users of hospital-based settings often have to wait longer to be seen than do users of physicians' offices, clinics, or health maintenance organizations (HMOs). They may see a different provider each time they visit, which may cost the system more in the long-run because of the lack of a patient-provider relationship to aid in determining the appropriateness of the visit. One study of a municipal hospital reported that patients without a regular doctor used fewer services and delayed their admission to the hospital (Weissman et al. 1991). The study also suggested that these delays may lead to different outcomes in the treatment of congestive heart failure, asthma, or cancer. In another study, having a primary care provider as a gatekeeper to inpatient and outpatient services or using a primary care team resulted in decreased use of ER services among regular users of ERs (Hochheiser, Woodward, and Charney 1971; Hurley, Freund, and Taylor 1989). Other studies note that doctors who have an ongoing relationship with their patients are less likely to duplicate work previously performed, less likely to require unnecessary laboratory tests, and less likely to require an office visit when a less expensive telephone consultation would suffice (Breslau and Haug 1976; Starfield et al. 1976; Breslau and Reeb 1975; Heagarty et al. 1970). Doctors with this type of relationship are also more likely to state that the results of the care they provided were closer to their expectations (Becker, Dracchman, and Kirscht 1974; Hayward et al. 1991).

Given the importance of a strong doctor-patient relationship, why are some individuals so reliant on hospital-based care? The factors correlated with reliance on OPD use, as well as those that best explain the preference for using OPDs, both for initial visits and for repeated use, will be examined here.

DATA AND METHODS

The data used in this paper are from the household component of the 1987 National Medical Expenditure Survey (NMES) (Edwards and Berlin 1989). NMES uses a national probability sample of the U.S. civilian noninstitutionalized population to provide nationally representative estimates of health-care use and expenditures for the period January 1 to December 31, 1987. (See Appendix for a description of the survey.)

The analyses in this paper are based on data collected using three questionnaires administered in the household survey: a health status questionnaire, a questionnaire concerning individuals' usual source of care, and an extensive questionnaire on sociodemographic, medical, and insurance characteristics during calendar year 1987. Questions regarding the usual source of care—to determine whether the respondent had a usual source, the type of source, and waiting time at the source—were administered in a special supplement to the household survey.

Each person was classified according to the total 1987 income of his or her family (family membership as of the fourth interview). Personal income from all family members was summed to obtain family income. Within a household, all individuals related by blood, marriage, adoption, or foster care status were considered members of a family. Poverty status was determined by the ratio of family income to the poverty levels published by the Bureau of the Census, controlling for family size and age of head of family. The poverty line for a single individual was $5,778 in 1987, while it was $11,611 for a family of four and $23,105 for a family of nine persons (US Bureau of the Census 1992). Thus, a single person who earned less than $5,778 in 1987 was considered to be living in poverty.

Classification by racial/ethnic background was based on information reported for each household member. Categories were those defined by the Office of Management and Budget and used in the 1980 and 1990 censuses. Respondents were asked if their racial backgrounds were best described as American Indian, Alaska Native, Asian or Pacific Islander, black (African American), white, or other. They also were asked if their main national origin or ancestry was among the following Hispanic subpopulations, regardless of racial background: Puerto Rican; Cuban; Mexican; Mexicano, Mexican American, or Chicano; other Latin American; or other Hispanic. The category of African American used here includes only persons of African ancestry who are not also Hispanic.

An important caveat should be noted. It has been previously suggested that researchers should examine the variations that exist among a heterogeneous population such as Hispanics (Schur, Bernstein, and Berk 1987). However, even with oversampling, the small sample size in NMES for the Hispanic subpopulations who use an OPD precludes an analysis of variations among Puerto Ricans, Mexicans, Cubans, or other Hispanics.

The insurance data presented in this report were based on data collected in the last round of the survey. Questions were asked to determine whether a person was covered on the interview date by Medicare, Medicaid, other public assistance that pays for medical care, CHAMPUS/CHAMPVA, or private health insurance. Persons without coverage from any of these sources during this round were defined as uninsured.

Measures of the use of services were based on the reports provided by the respondents during each round (parents provided the data for their children). OPD visits were any visits to a hospital outpatient department that did not result in a hospital admission or an overnight stay in the hospital.

One of the major purposes of NMES is to allow for the construction of population estimates based on sample data. Since the statistics presented in this paper are based on a sample, they may differ somewhat from the figures that would have been obtained if a complete census had been taken. This potential difference between sample results and a complete count is the sampling error of the estimate. Tests of statistical significance were used to determine whether differences between population estimates exist at specified levels of confidence or whether they simply occurred by chance. Differences were tested using Z-scores having asymptotic normal properties, based on the rounded figures at the 0.05 level of significance. Unless otherwise noted, only statistically significant differences between estimates are discussed in the text.

CHARACTERISTICS OF THOSE WHO USE OPDs

Hispanics and African Americans who were regular users of OPDs were compared to those who were regular users of physician's offices by sociodemographic factors, measures of health status, and the convenience of care. As reflected by the indicators of the convenience of services at the usual source of care (table 5.1), an OPD has several advantages over a physician's office, clinic, or HMO for both African Americans and Hispanics. The OPD allows greater flexibility in arranging for needed care. African Americans who used OPDs were more likely than African Americans who used physicians' offices to obtain care on weekday evenings (30.6% vs. 23.5%) and during the weekend (other than Saturday mornings) (17.2 vs. 6.9%) (table 5.1). They were also more likely to see a provider without an appointment (35.1% vs. 23.8%), i.e., "walks in or only sometimes has an appointment."

While the primary advantage of the OPD is the flexibility in arranging for care, the price of this scheduling flexibility is the lack of prompt care. Almost 30 percent (27.7%) of the African Americans who regularly used OPDs waited more than one hour to be seen by a medical provider; only 10 percent for African Americans who regularly went to a physicians' office waited this long. At the same time, African Americans who used OPDs typically waited longer for their scheduled visit (more than one week after scheduling an appointment) than did users of physicians' offices.

The differences found in the convenience of services for African Americans were consistent for Hispanics as well. Hispanics who regularly used OPDs were more likely to find the setting open for emergency care after hours, in the evenings, and during the weekend (after Saturday mornings) than were regular users of physicians' offices. However, Hispanic OPD users were likely to wait longer to be seen than users of physicians' offices.

There is one other striking pattern for both Hispanics and African Americans. No statistically significant difference was found in the length of time they were affiliated with their usual source of care (table 5.1). Close to two-thirds of the African Americans stated they were regular users of OPDs or physicians' offices for more than two years. Similarly, the majority of Hispanics stated they were regular users of OPDs or physicians' offices for more than two years. So it seems that contrary to commonly accepted belief, the lack of affiliation with a usual source of care was not a factor in the choice of the OPD for care.

Aside from the relationships noted regarding the convenience of care, there was some evidence that suggested that OPDs serve different segments of the African American and Hispanic populations (table 5.2). Among African Americans who used OPDs, 37 percent were poor, while the remainder were low- and middle/upper-income. At the same time, only 30 percent of the African Americans who used OPDs had any private insurance. The other 70 percent of the users were uninsured or had only public insurance. The vast majority (92.2 percent) of the African Americans who used OPDs lived in urban or suburban areas of the country. Finally, a large portion (74.2%) of African Americans who regularly used OPDs reported themselves to be in good or excellent health.

Like African Americans, a large portion of Hispanics who were regular users of OPDs lacked private insurance and resided in urban areas (table 5.2). However, OPDs served a larger proportion of middle- and upper-income Hispanics than of African Americans at these economic levels. Close to 60 percent of the Hispanics who were regular users of OPDs were uninsured or had only public insurance. As in the case of African Americans, slightly over 92 percent of the Hispanics who were regular users of OPDs lived in urban or suburban areas. Finally, over 80 percent (81.6%) of the Hispanics who were regular users of OPDs reported themselves as being in good or excellent health.

The descriptive findings suggest that lack of insurance may be a factor in the use of this care for middle- or upper-income Hispanics and African Americans. On the surface, the convenience of services may also be a factor in the regular use of OPDs for these groups.

The combined influence of these factors on the use of ambulatory care is examined below.

LIKELIHOOD OF USING AN OPD

The relative likelihood (logistic regression results) of using an outpatient department clinic among Hispanics and African Americans was evaluated using multivariate analyses (table 5.3). These multivariate models incorporate measures of the convenience and financing of care, as well as other sociodemographic factors related to the use of medical services.

For African Americans, gender, usual source of care, and health status were significantly correlated with the decision to use an OPD for ambulatory medical services. For African Americans, regular users of emergency rooms were less likely than individuals with no usual source of care to make at least one visit to the outpatient clinic for their medical needs. However, African Americans who reported an outpatient clinic as their usual source of care were just as likely as those without a usual source of care to make a visit to an OPD. At the same time, African American females were less likely than African American males to initiate an OPD visit. Finally, African Americans in fair or poor health were less likely than others to visit an OPD.

For Hispanics, regular users of physicians' offices or OPDs were less likely than individuals with no usual source of care to initiate an ambulatory visit to an OPD. Furthermore, Hispanics who had a regular doctor as their usual source of care were less likely than their counterparts with no usual source of care to visit an OPD. As in the case of African Americans, however, the perceived health status of Hispanics was correlated with the decision to visit an OPD. Hispanics in fair or poor health were less likely than others to initiate a visit to an OPD.

Many believe that the decision to seek ambulatory care should be seen as a separate issue from the amount of care received after entering the system. For example, in other research on access to care for African Americans and Hispanics, insurance, health status, and other factors were predictors of the decision to visit a provider, but only health status was predictive of the amount of care received after the initial ambulatory visit (Cornelius 1991). An examination was conducted regarding the decision to initiate an ambulatory visit to an OPD, as well as the number of visits to a hospital clinic for those who visited an OPD during the year. As reported in table 5.4, the most significant predictor of the number of visits to an OPD, controlling for health insurance, the convenience of care, and other factors, was having an OPD as a usual source of care. While a second influencing factor for African Americans was their perceived health status, this did not influence the number of visits to OPDs by Hispanics.

CONCLUSIONS AND POLICY IMPLICATIONS

On the surface, a multitude of factors were related to the use of OPDs by African Americans. African Americans and Hispanics who regularly use OPDs reported these settings as being more flexible in terms of their availability, that is, open for more days and times. These settings also served a considerable portion of African Americans and Hispanics who had public insurance or who were uninsured, as well as those who saw themselves as being in good or excellent health.

However, when a range of factors that influence the use of hospital OPDs are examined, a different pattern emerges. First, while OPDs served a significant portion of those who were uninsured or who had public insurance, the availability of insurance was not the primary factor in their decision to go to an OPD. Perceived health status and the type of usual source of care were consistently related to the decision to use an OPD. Second, while a significant portion of individuals stated they regularly used OPDs because of the convenience of services in this setting, this did not significantly influence the decision of African Americans and Hispanics to seek care there. Finally, the type of usual source of care (hospital emergency rooms for African Americans and physicians' offices as well as OPDs for Hispanics) and the presence of a regular doctor at the usual source of care for Hispanics, played a role in the use of ambulatory care at OPDs for these groups. This role varied in terms of the decision to initiate a visit to an OPD versus the decision to continue using an OPD after the first visit. Regardless of the factors that influenced the decision to initiate a visit to an OPD, having an OPD as a usual source of care was significantly related to the decision to keep returning there for medical treatment.

The results indicate that the use of OPDs is primarily related to the health status and type of usual source of care of the respondent. The finding that African Americans and Hispanics who are regular users of hospital-based ambulatory care report more visits to OPDs than others might suggest that these settings have an investment in perpetuating the use of hospital-based ambulatory care. However, more work on provider referral patterns is needed to determine whether hospital-based ambulatory care settings tend to refer patients to their own type of setting for follow-up care.

The fact that insurance status was not significantly related to the continued use of care in this setting suggests that changes in the financing of care, in and of themselves, may not lead to changes in the dependency on hospital-based ambulatory care. Changing the dependency of African Americans and Hispanics on hospital-based ambulatory care may require the development and implementation of incentives that encourage patients and providers to seek alternative settings when the need for initial or follow-up care arises.

REFERENCES

Aday, L.A., G. Fleming, and R. Andersen. 1984. *Access to Medical Care in the U.S.: Who Has It, Who Doesn't.* Chicago: Pluribus Press.

Andersen, R.M., L.A. Aday, C.S. Lyttle, L.J. Cornelius, and M.S. Chen. 1987. *Ambulatory Care and Insurance Coverage in an Era of Constraint.* Chicago: Pluribus Press.

Becker, M.H., R.H. Dracchman, and J.P. Kirscht. 1974. A field experiment to evaluate various outcomes of continuity of physician care. *American Journal of Public Health* 64:1062.

Blendon, R.J., L.H. Aiken, H.E. Freeman, and C.R. Corey. 1989. Access to medical care for black and white Americans: A matter of continuing concern. *Journal of the American Medical Association* 261:278-281.

Breslau, N., and M.R. Haug. 1976. Service delivery structure and continuity of care: A cases study of pediatric practice in the process of re-organization. *The Journal of Health and Social Behavior* 17:339.

Breslau, N., and K.G. Reeb. 1975. Continuity of care in a university-based practice. *Journal of Medical Education* 50:596.

Cornelius, L.J. 1993a. Barriers of access to care for white, black and Hispanic children. *Journal of the National Medical Association* 85(4).

Cornelius, L.J. 1993b. Ethnic minorities and access to medical care: Where do they stand? *Journal of the American Association of Minority Physicians* 4(1).

Cornelius, L.J. 1991. Access to medical care for black Americans with an episode of illness. *Journal of the National Medical Association* 83(7):617-626.

Cornelius, L.J., K. Beauregard, and J. Cohen. 1991. *Usual Sources of Medical Care and Their Characteristics.* DHHS pub. no. (PHS) 91-0042. Rockville, MD: US Department of Health and Human Services.

Edwards, W.S., and M. Berlin. 1989. *Questionnaires and Data Collection Methods for the Household Survey and the Survey of American Indians and Alaska Natives.* National Medical Expenditure Survey: Method, No. 2. DHHS pub. no. (PHS) 89-3450. Rockville, MD: US Department of Health and Human Services, Public Health Service.

Fleming, G., and R.M. Andersen. 1986. *The Municipal Health Services Program: Improving Access While Controlling Costs?* Chicago: Pluribus Press.

Hayward, R.A., A.M. Bernard, H.E. Freeman, and C.R. Corey. 1991. Regular source of ambulatory care and access to health services. *American Journal of Public Health* 81(4):434-438.

Heagarty, M.C., L.S. Robertson, J. Kasa, and J.J. Alpert. 1970. Some comparative costs in comprehensive versus fragmented pediatric care. *Pediatrics* 46:596.

Hochheiser, L.I., K. Woodward, and E. Charney. 1971. Effects of the neighborhood health center on the use of pediatric emergency departments in Rochester, New York. *New England Journal of Medicine* 285:148-152.

Hurley, R.E, D.A. Freund, and D.R. Taylor. 1989. Emergency room use and primary care case management: Evidence from four Medicaid demonstration programs. *American Journal of Public Health* 79:843-846.

Link, C.R., S.H. Long, and R.F. Settle. 1982. Access to medical care: Differentials by race. *Journal of Health, Health Politics, Policy, and Law* 7(Summer):345-365.

Schur, C.L., A.B. Bernstein, and M.L. Berk. 1987. The importance of distinguishing Hispanic subpopulations in the use of medical care. *Medical Care* 25(7):627-641.

Short, P.F., L.J. Cornelius, and D.E. Goldstone. 1990. Health insurance of minorities in the United States. *Health Care for the Poor and Underserved* 1:9-24.

Starfield, B.H., D.W. Simborg, S.D. Horn, and S.A. Yourtee. 1976. Continuity and coordination: Their achievement and utility. *Medical Care* 14:625-636.

Suarez, Z. 1988. A study of the use of self-care and outpatient medical care by Latinos in Chicago. Doctoral Dissertation, University of Chicago, School of Social Service Administration.

US Bureau of the Census. 1992. *Statistical Abstract of the United States, 1991.* Washington, DC: Government Printing Office.

Weissman, J.S., et al. 1991. Delayed access to health care: Risk factors, reasons and consequences. *Annals of Internal Medicine* 114(4): 325-331.

Yelin, H., J.S. Kramer, and W.V. Epstein. 1983. Is health care use equivalent among social groups? A diagnosis-based study. *American Journal of Public Health* 73(May):563-571.

Table 5.1
Convenience of services for those who regularly use a doctor's office or hospital outpatient department/clinic (OPD) by race/ethnicity, 1987
(In percents)

	AFRICAN AMERICANS		HISPANICS	
	Doctor's office users	Hospital OPD users	Doctor's office users	Hospital OPD users
CONVENIENCE OF SERVICES AT SOURCE OF CARE				
Evening hours	23.5	30.6	24.1	42.7
Saturday hours	41.5	34.1	51.9	49.4
Other weekend hours	6.9	17.2	10.9	30.0
SERVICES PROVIDED AT SOURCE				
Emergency care after hours	61.6	67.1	58.0	70.2
LENGTH OF TIME WITH REGULAR SOURCE				
Less than 1 year	20.0	17.6	23.4	24.6
1–2 years	13.0	11.9	14.6	17.6
More than 2 years	62.7	63.9	59.1	54.4
MAKES APPOINTMENT				
Has appointment	75.6	63.6	64.7	49.4
Walks in	13.2	21.9	21.8	24.7
Sometimes has an appointment	10.6	13.2	12.6	26.0
WAITING TIME BEFORE SEEING DOCTOR				
1–2 days	47.6	28.4	51.8	33.9
3–8 days	35.9	31.5	28.0	34.6
9–30 days	6.7	18.2	5.8	13.4
31 days or more	2.5	15.5	5.2	11.5
WAITING TIME AT SOURCE TO SEE PROVIDER				
Less than 30 minutes	74.9	53.0	70.6	56.4
30–59 minutes	5.4	7.8	5.5	2.4
60 minutes or more	10.0	27.7	17.1	32.8

Continued on next page

Table 5.1 continued

	AFRICAN AMERICANS		HISPANICS	
	Doctor's office users	Hospital OPD users	Doctor's office users	Hospital OPD users
TOTAL VISIT TIME AT SOURCE				
Less than 30 minutes	33.2	19.6	31.9	21.3
30–59 minutes	18.2	12.2	16.4	14.6
60 minutes or more	45.9	63.5	48.3	57.7

SOURCE: 1987 National Medical Expenditure Survey
NOTE: Columns may not add to 100 percent because of item non-response.

Table 5.2
Characteristics of those who regularly use a doctor's office or hospital outpatient department/clinic (OPD) by race/ethnicity, 1987

CHARACTERISTICS	AFRICAN AMERICANS		HISPANICS	
	Doctor's office users	Hospital OPD users	Doctor's office users	Hospital OPD users
AGE (percent)				
Under 15	31.2	28.5	34.0	37.8
15–18	8.5	7.4	7.3	5.9
19–24	9.0	11.1	10.4	7.3
25–44	30.9	33.0	31.9	32.4
45–64	20.4	20.0	16.4	16.6
INCOMEA (percent)				
Poor	29.8	37.0	23.1	28.9
Low income	21.3	26.7	26.7	29.6
Middle/high income	48.9	36.3	49.9	41.5
HEALTH INSURANCE B (percent)				
Any private	59.1	30.0	54.8	40.6
Only public	24.2	44.1	16.5	20.3
Uninsured	16.7	25.9	28.7	39.1
EDUCATIONC (percent)				
Less than 12 years	33.0	32.6	43.8	47.0
12 years	35.5	39.9	28.5	30.1
More than 12 years	30.2	26.1	25.7	19.6
AREA OF RESIDENCE (percent)				
19 largest SMSAs	29.5	41.4	34.4	55.9
Other SMSAs	42.3	50.8	43.2	36.5
Non-SMSA	28.2	7.8	22.4	7.6
REGION OF RESIDENCE (percent)				
Northeast	16.3	15.5	13.7	27.7
Midwest	17.6	23.6	9.3	11.3
South	58.8	46.8	38.9	16.8
West	7.3	14.2	38.1	44.2

Continued on next page

Table 5.2 continued

CHARACTERISTICS	AFRICAN AMERICANS		HISPANICS	
	Doctor's office users	Hospital OPD users	Doctor's office users	Hospital OPD users
SELF-REPORTED HEALTH STATUS *(percent)*				
Fair/poor	20.8	25.8	19.0	18.4
Good/excellent	79.2	74.2	81.0	81.6
DISABILITY DAYS				
Mean bed disability days D	12.2	20.1	9.2	12.9
Mean work loss disability days E	11.6	16.2	12.0	6.7

SOURCE: 1987 National Medical Expenditure Survey
NOTE: Columns may not add to 100 percent because of item non-response.
A Poor = Under 1.0 x Poverty (included those with negative income); Low income = 1.0–1.99 x Poverty; Middle/high income = 2.0 x Poverty and greater
B Insurance coverage during the last quarter of 1987
C Education level of adults
D For those with at least one bed disability day
E For those with at least one work loss disability day

Table 5.3
Relative odds of visiting a hospital outpatient department (log-odds) by race/ethnicity, 1987

POPULATION CHARACTERISTICS	AFRICAN AMERICANS N=5,519	HISPANICS N=2,825
AGE A	0.83	0.98
GENDER		
Female	0.69***	0.55
Male	Reference group	Reference group
CONVENIENCE OF SERVICES AT SOURCE OF CARE		
Evening hours	0.89	1.20
Weekend hours	0.95	0.52
Saturday hours	1.16	1.17
Emergency after hours	0.90	0.99
Weekday hours only	Reference group	Reference group
INCOME		
Poor	1.02	0.87
Near-poor/low income	1.08	1.11
Middle/high income	Reference group	Reference group
USUAL SOURCE OF CARE		
Doctor's office	1.10	0.90***
Hospital outpatient clinic	0.19	0.14***
Emergency room	0.67***	—
Other site	0.53	0.63 B
None	Reference group	Reference group
REGULAR DOCTOR		
Regular doctor at usual source of care	0.68	0.72*
No regular doctor at usual source of care	Reference group	Reference group
HEALTH STATUS		
Fair/poor perceived health	0.55*	0.50*
Good/excellent perceived health	Reference group	Reference group
BED DISABILITY DAYS A	0.99	0.99

Continued on next page

Table 5.3 continued

POPULATION CHARACTERISTICS	AFRICAN AMERICANS N=5,519	HISPANICS N=2,825
HEALTH INSURANCE		
Public insurance	0.68	1.02
Uninsured	1.27	1.87
Private insurance	Reference group	Reference group
REGION OF RESIDENCE		
Midwest	1.06	1.42
South	1.10	2.68
West	0.90	1.62
Northeast	Reference group	Reference group
AREA OF RESIDENCE		
SMSA	0.83	1.06
Non-SMSA	Reference group	Reference group
YEARS OF COMPLETED EDUCATION A	0.97	0.92
INTERCEPT	3.35***	3.50***
GAMMA (γ)	0.45	0.52

SOURCE: 1987 National Medical Expenditure Survey
A Continuous variable
B Emergency room and other site were combined.
$*p < 0.05$ $***p < 0.001$

Table 5.4
Parameter estimates: Number of visits in hospital outpatient departments by race/ethnicity, 1987

POPULATION CHARACTERISTICS	AFRICAN AMERICANS N=5,519	HISPANICS N=2,825
AGE A	0.0152	0.0030
GENDER		
Female	-0.0912	-0.0345
Male	Reference group	Reference group
CONVENIENCE OF SERVICES AT SOURCE OF CARE		
Evening hours	0.0573	-0.1010
Weekend hours	-0.7300	-0.0020
Saturday hours	0.2819	-0.1675
Emergency after hours	-0.0053	0.1641
Weekday hours only	Reference group	Reference group
INCOME		
Poor	-0.0139	0.0374
Near-poor/low income	0.1020	0.0532
Middle/high income	Reference group	Reference group
USUAL SOURCE OF CARE		
Doctor's office	-0.3754	0.0974
Hospital outpatient clinic	2.2937**	1.7871*
Emergency room	0.2696	0.0001
Other site	0.3557	0.1289
None	Reference group	Reference group
REGULAR DOCTOR		
Regular doctor at usual source of care	0.2703	-0.1174
No regular doctor at usual source of care	Reference group	Reference group
HEALTH STATUS		
Fair/poor perceived health	0.7378**	0.2300
Good/excellent perceived health	Reference group	Reference group
BED DISABILITY DAYS A	0.0232	0.0206

Continued on next page

Table 5.4 continued

POPULATION CHARACTERISTICS	AFRICAN AMERICANS $N=5,519$	HISPANICS $N=2,825$
HEALTH INSURANCE		
Public insurance	0.5458	0.1999
Uninsured	-0.2877	-0.1593
Private insurance	Reference group	Reference group
REGION OF RESIDENCE		
Midwest	-0.3334	-0.3044
South	0.2438	-0.4134
West	0.1114	-0.2851
Northeast	Reference group	Reference group
AREA OF RESIDENCE		
SMSA	0.4801	0.0991
Non-SMSA	Reference group	Reference group
YEARS OF COMPLETED EDUCATION[A]	-0.0526	0.0202
INTERCEPT	-0.1759	0.0624
R^2	0.0590	0.1120

SOURCE: 1987 National Medical Expenditure Survey
[A] Continuous variable
$^*p < 0.05$ $^{**}p < 0.01$

A Comparison of Financial, Access, and Sociocultural Barriers to Care Among Hypertensives Across Three Ethnic Groups

Christine A. Stroup-Benham and Linda C. Perkowski

Barriers to medical care pose a kaleidoscope of problems for the health-care consumer, particularly those who are financially or socially disadvantaged. Minorities and persons living below the poverty level are at particular risk for not having adequate access to health care due to conditions such as lack of health insurance, lack of a cross-cultural match between the medical care provider and the consumer, and living in an area with insufficient medical resources. This situation is particularly risky for persons with chronic diseases such as hypertension since these barriers may reduce the likelihood of early detection and effective continuity of treatment.

This investigation addresses the question, "What are the financial, access, and sociocultural barriers to health care among black, Hispanic, and white hypertensives?" and compares these barriers to health care among hypertensives across the three racial/ethnic groups. Financial barriers, including poverty status, employment status, and health insurance coverage (e.g., private, Medicare, CHAMPUS, CHAMPVA, Medicaid, or other public assistance) are examined first. The second group of barriers include are access barriers: existence of a usual source of care, mode of transportation to source of care, travel time to source, amount of time until appointment, and length of time spent waiting in doctor's office. Sociocultural barriers include the doctor's gender, the racial/ethnic background of the usual physician, the patient's perception of his global health status, and the ability of the doctor to speak the patient's native language. In addition, this research explores the health care received by these hypertensive individuals through their reports of number of physician visits and whether or not they have had their blood pressure checked.

LITERATURE REVIEW

Hypertension is one of the most common health conditions in America, but its prevalence varies among races/ethnicities (Drizol, Danneberg, and Engel 1986). Studies have indicated that blacks are at particular risk for this disease, compared to whites and Hispanics (Schneiderman 1992). Hypertension is more prevalent among blacks than whites, even after controlling for socioeconomic factors, age, and obesity (Adams-Campbell, Brambilla, and McKinlay 1993; HDFP Cooperative Group 1977; Cassel et al. 1971). Similar or lower prevalence rates have been reported for Hispanics compared to non-Hispanic Whites (Haffner et al. 1992; Franco et al. 1985). These rates are in contradiction to the risk profiles of Mexican Americans, which reflect a prevalence of obesity and poverty more comparable to blacks than to whites (Sorel, Ragland, and Syme 1991). Thus, higher rates of hypertensives would be expected among Mexican Americans.

Hypertension is a major risk factor for cardiovascular and cerebrovascular disease, which are major contributors to morbidity and mortality in the elderly, particularly in blacks (Dunn and Pringle 1991; Lackland et al. 1992; Gillum 1991; Svetkey et al. 1993). Early detection and effective treatment of this condition reduce these negative health outcomes, therefore, controlling hypertension and modifying risk factors are significant health promotion objectives (Wilcox and Mosher 1993).

Both the public and physicians are becoming better educated about hypertension, resulting in a decrease in the incidence of stroke and heart disease (Roccella and Horan 1988; Goldman and Cook 1984; Ostfeld and Wilk 1990; Thom and Maurer 1988). However, hypertension control among minority populations, those living in poverty, individuals with lower educational levels, and those with restricted access to medical care is still a significant health problem (Keeler et al. 1985; Kittner et al. 1990; Rostand et al., 1982). For example, coronary heart disease remains one of the major causes of morbidity and mortality for blacks (Gillum 1982).

Because access to health care is critical for appropriate prevention, detection, and treatment, delineation of barriers to care is a necessary first step to direct planning of health-care policy. Lack of adequate access to medical care is due to a variety of factors, including absence of health-care insurance, insufficient or inaccessible medical resources, and cultural, gender, and language barriers between health-care provider and client. These factors impinge upon racial/ethnic groups to different degrees. Treviño and Moss (1983) reported that blacks, Puerto Ricans, and Cuban Americans were at least twice as likely as whites to be without medical care insurance, while Mexican Americans were 3.5 times as likely as whites to be uninsured. Similar findings are reported with Hispanics generally, indicating less access to health care and higher premiums for medical care coverage than whites (Cornelius 1993; Hubbell et al. 1991; Valdez et al. 1993). In addition, it has been suggested that poor Hispanics are the most likely to be impacted by medical care costs (Andersen, Giachello, and Aday 1986). Blacks are also less likely than whites to have received necessary supportive services, such as medications and supplies (Hayward et al. 1988).

Delays in receiving medical care may also be considered a barrier to health care. Such delays may be experienced at several points in the process of health-care acquisition. The patient may delay seeking care for a variety of reasons, including lack of knowledge about the condition, lack of understanding of treatment regimen, and financial concerns (Hackett, Cassem, and Raker 1973; Temoshok et al. 1984). Delayed access to care appears to be experienced differentially by subpopulations. Weissman and associates (1991) stated that more than 20 percent of patients who were uninsured, poor, black, or without a regular source of care reported delays. Collectively, such delays may ultimately affect early diagnosis, the severity of the condition, and the cost of treatment.

Cultural and language barriers have been reported as impediments to health-care access for Hispanics (Treviño, Stroup, and Ray 1991; Lewin-Epstein 1991). The patient's lack of fluency in English and the physician's inability to converse in the patient's native language can result in misunderstandings regarding diagnoses, treatment, and patient education. Such misunderstandings interfere with provision of and access to health care (Haffner 1992). Anthropologists have attempted to determine the culturally specific sets through which various ethnic groups perceive and report their physical symptoms (Angel and Guarnaccia 1989). How these cultural differences influence the patient's perception of health-care needs and, thus, the provision of health care have not been established.

Many researchers have explored the relationship between the gender of the patient and that of the health-care provider (West 1993; Delgado, Lopez-Fernandez, and de Dios Luna 1993). Although there are no conclusive findings that gender consistently impacts upon patient satisfaction or quality of care (West 1993), Bishop (1992) argues that if a gender bias exists "such bias can affect the doctor/patient relationship on a conscious or unconscious level." This bias would influence the doctor/patient relationship and, therefore, could affect patient satisfaction or the ability or motivation of the patient to comply with the physician's orders (Delgado, Lopez-Fernandez, and de Dios Luna 1993).

In several major epidemiological studies, perceived health status has been demonstrated to be a significant predictor of mortality (Wolinsky and Johnson 1992; Idler and Angel 1990; Idler and Kasl 1991; Idler, Kasl, and Lemke 1990). Lower self-ratings of health status have been associated with lack of health insurance in several studies (Franks et al. 1993; Lurie et al. 1984; Patrick et al. 1992). Increased risk for poor health and lack of insurance are associated with similar socioeconomic factors such as fewer years of formal education and poverty (Feldman et al. 1989; House, Kessler, and Herzog 1990).

In this study, information is presented regarding the barriers encountered by those who have a definite need to have access to health care, namely, persons who have been told by a physician that they have high blood pressure. By exploring ethnic-specific barriers in access to care, population-specific policies may be designed and implemented to increase those individuals' use of medical care and thereby to reduce the risk for hypertension-related end diseases (e.g., heart and vascular diseases). Such actions would benefit both the patient and the health-care system.

METHODS

Data for this study were obtained from the 1987 National Medical Expenditure Survey (NMES), conducted by the Agency for Health Care Policy and Research. A complete description of the survey is provided by Edwards and Berlin (1989). (See also the description in the Appendix to this book.)

Sample weights were employed to produce population estimates. These weights were used to adjust for the sampling procedures used to oversample the above-mentioned population segments. All analyses were performed both unweighted and weighted, and the weighted results are presented unless otherwise stated. Normalized sample weights were used so that the resultant p-values were not inflated. The reported sample variances have been adjusted for design effects by using the statistical program SESUDAAN (which uses the Taylor approximation method).

Descriptive analyses, including frequencies and univariates, of the aforementioned variables for each racial/ethnic group were computed, both unweighted and weighted. Then a comparison of the weighted results for the three racial/ethnic groups via chi-squares (for categorical variables) and analyses of variance (ANOVAs) (for continuous variables) were conducted. The results of these analyses are provided in the following section.

The inclusionary criteria for this investigation were: (1) being identified as a Key Person of the non-institutionalized households in the NMES, (2) being age 18 to 64 years, inclusive, (3) answering affirmatively to the question Has a doctor ever told you that you had high blood pressure? (hypertension), and (4) being identified as either African American (black non-Hispanic), Hispanic, or non-Hispanic white. After these criteria were applied to the population, a final sample of 3,515 resulted: 987 blacks, 277 Hispanics, and 2,251 non-Hispanic whites were included in our analyses. This sample represented approximately 12 percent of the total NMES sample of non-Hispanic whites, blacks, and Hispanics.

Several sociodemographic variables were used in our analyses, including gender, age, and marital status. Education was examined both as a continuous variable as well as a categorical variable. The categorical version was a trichotomous variable designed so that 0 to 8 years of education were coded as 1; 9 to 11 years were coded as 2; and 12 or more years were coded as 3. Marital status included five response categories: never married, married, separated, divorced, and widowed.

Financial Barriers

A variety of variables were examined to assess financial barriers to care. Employment status was a dichotomous variable reflecting whether or not the individual was currently employed. Poverty level was also dichotomous, reflecting at or below poverty level versus above poverty level. Health insurance coverage was coded as private, public (including Medicare, Medicaid, and CHAMPUS/CHAMPVA), or none.

Barriers to Access

First, it was determined whether individuals had a usual source of medical care and in what location care was provided. Locations included: doctor's office, doctor's clinic, family health center, hospital outpatient clinic, company clinic, school clinic, hospital emergency room, walk-in center, patient's home, or HMO. Second, the mode of transportation to the source of health care was examined. Data was collected in several categories: walking, driving, driven by another individual, taxi, other public transportation, or visited by the doctor in one's home.

Third, time variables were assessed, including (1) travel time in minutes to source of care, (2) amount of time, in days, until appointment, and (3) length of time, in minutes, spent waiting in the doctor's office.

Sociocultural Barriers

The sociocultural barriers examined in this study were based on the language, ethnicity, and gender of the individual and of the physician. A proxy measure of the language barrier to care was created by combining two variables, the patient's native language and the ability of the doctor to speak the patient's native language. Matches between patient and doctor gender and race/ethnicity were also determined. Since the ability of the individual to seek medical care is related to his perception of his own health needs, individuals self-reported global health status was examined. A four-point self-assessment of health was used, ranging from 1 = Excellent to 4 = Poor.

Care Received

To obtain an indication of the individual's use of medical care, two proxy measures were included. First, number of physician visits indicates medical care received by individuals, so this variable was investigated. Second, whether or not the individual has had his or her blood pressure checked was used to assess monitoring of hypertension.

RESULTS

The weighted sociodemographic information for hypertensives in each of the three racial/ethnic groups shows several differences among these groups. (Table 6.1.) First, the proportion of males was greatest among the whites and least among blacks. Second, the white subsample was older than both of the other ethnicities, although the only significant difference was between whites and Hispanics ($p < .01$). Third, the greatest percentage of married individuals was found among whites, while blacks had the lowest percentage. Additionally, the proportion of never-married individuals was nearly twice as high for blacks and Hispanics as for whites, while the proportion separated among blacks was about seven times that of whites and more than three times that of Hispanics. Finally, the mean number of years of education was highest for whites and lowest for Hispanics.

A variety of financial barriers were encountered by each of the racial/ethnic groups of hypertensives included in this investigation. Table 6.2 summarizes the results of the weighted analyses of financial barriers. More than half of each racial/ethnic group was employed; however, Hispanics had the greatest share of unemployed persons (45.76%). In addition, the percentage of individuals living at or below the poverty level was highest for blacks (29.41%). The poverty rate was also high among Hispanic individuals, (25.07%). These proportions are in strong contrast to the 8.20 percent of white individuals who reported being at or below the poverty level.

As expected in this group of hypertensives, whites were much more likely to have private health insurance coverage than were blacks and Hispanics. The highest rate of being uninsured was found among Hispanics (29.74%), whose rate was nearly three times that of whites and nearly one-and-a-half times that of blacks. Blacks had the highest percentage of public insurance coverage, with a rate nearly twice that of Whites. Hispanics also had a high rate of public insurance usage, reporting more than 23 percent.

More than 87 percent of whites, 84 percent of blacks, and 75 percent of Hispanics reported that they had a usual source of care. Thus, one-quarter of the Hispanic self-identified hypertensives did not have a usual source of care, while about one-sixth of blacks and whites did not have one. Table 6.3 provides the percentages of all types of usual care reported, as well as the mode of transportation typically used to get to the source of care. The usual source of care for a majority of all racial/ethnic groups was a doctor's office or a group practice. More blacks and Hispanics than whites listed either a neighborhood/family health center or a hospital outpatient clinic as their regular source of care. Very few other types of usual source of care were reported by these hypertensives. Driving was the most often reported mode of transportation to source of care. However, whites were more likely than blacks and Hispanics to report driving. Being driven, the next most frequent response, was listed by 20.71 percent of blacks, 16.95 percent of Hispanics, and 8.25 percent of whites.

Health care received by individuals showed no significant differences across races/ethnicities. (Table 6.4.) Approximately 90 percent of all three groups reported having their blood pressure checked in the last year. Although Hispanics and blacks had smaller mean numbers of doctor visits than whites, the difference was not statistically significant.

Time barriers to care were examined next. Table 6.5 provides the weighted results of the analyses pertaining to these barriers for this group of individuals reporting high blood pressure. Hispanics had the longest travel time and length of time spent waiting in the doctor's office. In fact, the difference between Hispanic and white mean travel times was statistically significant ($p < .01$). White individuals were significantly different from Hispanics and blacks in mean length of time spent waiting in the doctor's office. Wait times were least among whites, while blacks and Hispanics experienced similar wait times. No significant differences across races/ethnicities were found for length of time until appointment. The average time for all groups ranged from 6 to 7 days.

Sociocultural barriers were the final type of barriers to be examined (table 6.6). As anticipated, significantly fewer Hispanic individuals reported English as their native language. Those for whom English wasn't the native language were more likely to state that they were not fluent in English. Among whites and Hispanics, other native languages included Spanish, German, Italian, French, Portuguese, Greek, Hungarian, Yiddish, Arabic, Norwegian, and Polish.

Of the 46 Hispanic individuals who indicated that they did not speak English, nearly two-fifths did not have a physician who spoke their native language. Although in this population of self-reported hypertensives, blacks and Hispanics more often obtained care from minority physicians than did whites, white physicians were still the majority caregivers for blacks and Hispanics. Since less than 10 percent of all physicians visited were female, it is not surprising that there was a low match between physician and patient gender.

The majority of the individuals rated their health as good or excellent (table 6.7). However, the highest percentage of individuals indicating poor or fair health was found for blacks and Hispanics. These two racial/ethnic groups were also less likely than whites to state that their health was excellent.

DISCUSSION

As these results indicate, there are a variety of barriers to health care for self-reported hypertensives of various racial/ethnic backgrounds. As was expected, overall, blacks and Hispanics reported more financial, access, and sociocultural barriers to care than did whites.

Financial Barriers

Hypertensive blacks and Hispanics in this study were far more likely than hypertensive whites to be unemployed, uninsured, and living at or below the poverty level. Even when public forms of health insurance are considered, a larger proportion of blacks and Hispanics than whites in this study remained uninsured. In fact, 11.37 percent of whites, 19.93 percent of blacks, and 29.74 percent of Hispanics were without health insurance. These rates are comparable to those found for the overall NMES population as well as to previous findings from other investigators (Treviño and Moss 1984).

Although in previous research Hispanics have demonstrated a lower hypertensive rate than whites of the same socioeconomic level, the level of hypertension control in Hispanics usually lags behind that of whites, especially for men (Franco et al. 1985; Stern et al. 1981). This could be due to sociocultural factors such as lack of information or language barriers (Hazuda et al. 1983). Woodlander and Himmelstein (1988) found that being uninsured was associated with lower use of preventive services. Given the value in prevention, early detection, and continuous monitoring of hypertension, decreased visits to a physician could worsen health outcomes for these patients.

Financial barriers of any kind are particularly significant for those with hypertension. Not only does such a chronic condition require continuous monitoring, which means more visits to the doctor, it also may necessitate several types of medications being prescribed (Ménard 1989). Both of these factors result in higher health-care costs to the patient. If patients do not have the financial resources or health insurance to pay for these costs, the long-term result is likely to be increased morbidity and mortality.

Barriers to Access to Health Care

Having a regular source of care and being able to get to that source are very important for persons with hypertension. This is particularly true for blacks since black hypertensives have been shown to have a greater incidence of cardiac enlargement and stroke and are at greater risk of end-stage renal disease and hypertensive renal disease than whites (HDFP Cooperative Group 1979a, 1979b, 1982; Rostand et al. 1982). More than 15 percent of blacks and 25 percent of Hispanics in this study did not have a regular source of care, indicating that their hypertension is probably not being monitored as it should be. Continuity of care is important with a chronic condition such as hypertension. In addition, the lack of a regular provider is problematic for any individual with a chronic condition, regardless of race/ethnicity.

The results regarding modes of transportation to source of care may be another indication of disparate access to care across races/ ethnicities. Blacks and Hispanics were much more likely than whites to report using a taxi or other form of public transportation to get to their source of care. Since this increases the overall cost of obtaining health care, this is particularly troublesome for those for whom financial considerations are an impediment to health care.

The results regarding percentage of individuals having their blood pressure checked in the previous year are similar to those for the total NMES population. More than 10 percent of the hypertensives reported not having their blood pressure checked in the past year, suggesting the lack of adequate medical supervision for their condition. In contrast, self-reported hypertensives reported having more doctors visits in the past year than did the overall NMES sample. As shown in table 6.4, hypertensive whites, blacks, and Hispanics made 4.5, 4.1, and 3.8 visits, respectively, compared to whites, blacks, and Hispanics in the overall sample, who made 3.4, 2.3, and 2.1 visits, respectively (data not shown). The latter results must be interpreted with caution since the reason for it is impossible to determine whether the number of visits is adequate for proper medical supervision of their condition.

Time Barriers to Care

Delays in receipt of health care were more often experienced by black and Hispanic individuals than by whites. These delays were in the form of travel time to source and time spent waiting in the doctor's office. Not only do such delays pose an inconvenience for the patient, they may negatively impinge in other ways. For instance, individuals may lose wages for time spent away from work, particularly those who do not have vacation or sick leave time available to them. Child-care providers must find someone to watch their children while they go to the doctor, take the children with them, or, in some cases, leave the children unattended. When such delays are experienced by those who are already disadvantaged, they add to the burden of trying to receive health care.

Sociocultural Barriers to Care

A variety of sociocultural health-care barriers were experienced by Hispanics. Few Hispanics spoke English as a native language, and a significant number were not fluent in English. If the physician is unable to converse with the patient in his/her native language, there are likely to be misunderstandings resulting in impediments to the provision of and access to care (Haffner 1992). The ability to communicate with the health-care provider is vital, particularly in a chronic condition such as hypertension that may require behavior modification and complex treatment regimens.

All three ethnicities experienced a low match between physician and individual gender. It has been reported by other researchers that gender does influence patient satisfaction with care (Bishop 1992). Such a gender bias may negatively impact the doctor/patient relationship, resulting in reduction of patient compliance with physician treatment plans or even reduced contact with the physician. All these consequences could adversely affect the health of those patients with hypertension.

Black and Hispanic hypertensives were more likely than whites to rate their health as fair to poor. This is hardly surprising since in this study these two populations also were poorer, less well educated, and more often lacking insurance than whites, all circumstances that would be likely to contribute to poorer health.

FUTURE DIRECTIONS FOR RESEARCH AND FOR POLICY REFORM

The present study is limited by its cross-sectional design. These results do not allow us to determine fully the nature of the relationship between hypertension status and access to health care. For example, although the results show that hypertensive blacks and Hispanics are more likely than whites to report that their health is fair or poor, they do not indicate whether this means that these groups are receiving inadequate care or even what factors might account for this differential. It also is not possible to conclude what effects longer waits for care by blacks and Hispanics might have on the quality of the care they receive or on their general health status. Further, the diagnosis of hypertension is based on self-reporting. Therefore, no data are available regarding the duration or severity of the hypertension or the adequacy of treatment. Although the results suggest that these hypertensive individuals had greater mean numbers of visits to a physician than the overall NMES population, this finding also must be interpreted with caution. Without specific data concerning physician visits for particular conditions, it is unknown if this reflects a true relationship between hypertensive status and contact with physician. It may be that these hypertensives have greater comorbidity and that the comorbid states trigger the greater number of physician visits.

Early identification and treatment of hypertension is crucial to improving outcomes for all racial/ethnic groups. Clearly, increasing the use of medical care would be one way to provide more opportunities for diagnosis and treatment of the disease. Studies indicate treatment of hypertension is beneficial at any age (SHEP Cooperative Research Group 1991). Consequently, policy reform directed at improving identification and treatment of hypertension among minority populations should focus on the removal of barriers that generally prevent or inhibit access to care for these groups. While financial impediments such as poverty and lack of health insurance coverage may be addressed through federal programs, resolving other access issues may require a multi-faceted response. As Hayward and associates (1988) have suggested, lack of health-care facilities, health-care professionals, and transportation in many poor, minority neighborhoods are as much barriers to access as "cultural and bureaucratic hostilities or outright discrimination that may set up institutional barriers to obtaining health care" (Funkhouser and Moser 1990). In fact, these barriers may be the biggest hurdles that remain in the quest for adequate health-care access for all races/ ethnicities.

REFERENCES

Adams-Campbell, L.L., D.J. Brambilla, and S.M. McKinlay. 1993. Corre-lates of the prevalence of self-reported hypertension among African-American and white women. *Ethnicity and Disease* 3:119-125.

Andersen R.M., A.L. Giachello, and L.A. Aday. 1986. Access of Hispanics to health care and cuts in services: A state of the art overview. *Public Health Reports* 101(3):238-252.

Angel, R., and P.J. Guarnaccia. 1989. Mind, body, and culture: Somatization among Hispanics. *Social Science and Medicine* 28(12):1229-1238.

Bishop, J. 1992. Guidelines for a non-sexist (gender-sensitive) doctor-patient relationship. *Canadian Journal of Psychiatry* 37:62-64.

Cassel, J., S. Heyden, A.G. Bartel, B.H. Kaplan, H.A. Tyroler, J.C. Cornoni, and C.G. Hanes. 1971. Incidence of coronary heart disease by ethnic group, social class, and sex. *Archives of Internal Medicine* 128:901.

Cornelius, L.J. 1993. Ethnic minorities and access to medical care: Where do they stand? *Journal of the Association for Academic Minority Physicians* 4(1):16-25.

Delgado, A., L.A. Lopez-Fernandez, and J. de Dios Luna. 1993. Influence of the doctor's gender in the satisfaction of the users. *Medical Care* 31(9):795-800.

Drizol, T., A.L. Danneberg, and A.B. Engel. 1986. Blood pressure levels in persons 18-74 years of age in 1976-80, and trends in blood pressure from 1960 to 1980 in the United States. *Vital and Health Statistics*, Series 11, No. 234. DHHS pub. no. (PHS) 86-1684. National Center for Health Statistics. Hyattsville, MD: Government Printing Office.

Dunn, F.G., and S.D. Pringle. 1991. Hypertension and coronary artery disease. Can the chain be broken? *Hypertension* 18:1126-1132.

Edwards, W.S., and M. Berlin. 1989. *Questionnaires and Data Collection Methods for the Household Survey and the Survey of American Indians and Alaska Natives*. National Medical Expenditure Survey: Method, No. 2. DHHS pub. no. (PHS) 89-3450. Rockville, MD: US Department of Health and Human Services, Public Health Service.

Feldman, J.J., D.M. Makuc, J.C. Kleinman, and J. Cornoni-Huntley. 1989. National trends in educational differentials in mortality. *American Journal of Epidemiology* 129:919-933.

Franco, L.J., M.P. Stern, M. Rosenthal, S.M. Haffner, H.P. Hazuda, and P.J. Comeaux. 1985. Prevalence, detection, and control of hypertension in a biethnic community: The San Antonio heart study. *American Journal of Epidemiology* 121(5):684-696.

Franks, P., C.M. Clancy, M.R. Gold, and P.A. Nutting. 1993. Health insurance and subjective health status. Data from the 1987 National Medical Expenditure Survey. *American Journal of Public Health* 83:1295-1299.

Funkhouser, S.W., and D.K. Moser. 1990. Is health care racist? *Advances in Nursing Science* 12(2):47-55.

Gillum, R.F. 1991. Cardiovascular disease in the United States: An epidemiologic overview. In *Cardiovascular Diseases in Blacks*, edited by E. Saunders, 9-16. Philadelphia: FA Davis Co.

Gillum R.F. 1982. Coronary heart disease in black populations, I: Mortality and morbidity. *American Heart Journal* 104:839-851.

Goldman, L., and E.F. Cook. 1984. The decline in ischemic heart disease mortality rates: An analysis of the comparative effects of medical interventions and changes in lifestyle. *Annals of Internal Medicine* 101:825-836.

Hackett, T.P., N.H. Cassem, and J.W. Raker. 1973. Patient delay in cancer. *New England Journal of Medicine* 289:14-20.

Haffner, L. 1992. Translation is not enough: Interpreting in a medical setting. *Western Journal of Medicine* 157(3):255-259.

Haffner, S.M., B.D. Mitchell, R.A. Valdez, H.P. Hazuda, P.A. Morales, and M.P. Stern. 1992. Eight-year incidence of hypertension in Mexican Americans and non-Hispanic whites: The San Antonio heart study. *American Journal of Hypertension* 5(3):147-153.

Hayward, R.A., M.F. Shapiro, H.E. Freeman, and C.R. Corey. 1988. Inequities in health services among insured Americans: Do working-age adults have less access to medical care than the elderly? *New England Journal of Medicine* 318(23):1507-1512.

Hazuda, H.P., M.P. Stern, S.P. Gaskill, S.M. Haffner, and L.I. Gardner. 1983. Ethnic differences in health knowledge and behaviors related to the prevention and treatment of coronary heart disease: The San Antonio heart study. *American Journal of Epidemiology* 117:717-728.

House, J.S., R.C. Kessler, and A.R. Herzog. 1990. Age, socioeconomic status, and health. *Milbank Quarterly* 68:383-411.

Hubbell, F.A., H. Waitzkin, S.I. Mishra, J. Dombrink, and L.R. Chavez. 1991. Access to medical care for documented and undocumented Latinos in a southern California county. *Western Journal of Medicine* 154(4):414-417.

Hypertensive Detection and Follow-up Program (HDFP) Cooperative Group. 1982. Five-year findings of the hypertension detection and follow-up program: III. *Journal of the American Medical Association* 247:633-638.

Hypertensive Detection and Follow-up Program (HDFP) Cooperative Group. 1979a. Five-year findings of the hypertension detection and follow-up program: I. *Journal of the American Medical Association* 242:2562-2571.

Hypertensive Detection and Follow-up Program (HDFP) Cooperative Group. 1979b. Five-year findings of the hypertension detection and follow-up program: II. *Journal of the American Medical Association* 242:2572-2577.

Hypertensive Detection and Follow-up Program (HDFP) Cooperative Group. 1977. Race, education and prevalence of hypertension. *American Journal of Epidemiology* 106:351-361.

Idler, E.L., and R. Angel. 1990. Self-rated health and mortality in the NHANES-I epidemiologic follow-up study. *American Journal of Public Health* 80:446-452.

Idler, E.L., and S. Kasl. 1991. Health perceptions and survival: Do global evaluations of health status really predict mortality? *Journal of Gerontology* 46:S55-S65.

Idler, E.L., S. Kasl, and J.H. Lemke. 1990. Self-evaluated health and mortality among the elderly in New Haven, Connecticut and Iowa and Washington Counties, Iowa. *Journal of Epidemiology* 131:91-103.

Keeler, E.B., R.H. Brook, G.A. Goldberg, C.J. Kamberg, and J.P. Newhouse. 1985. How free care reduced hypertension in the health insurance experiment. *Journal of the American Medical Association* 254:1926-1931.

Kittner, S.J., L.R. White, K.G. Losonczy, P.A. Wolf, and J.R. Hebel. 1990. Black-white differences in stroke incidence in a national sample: The contribution of hypertension and diabetes mellitus. *Journal of the American Medical Association* 264:1267-1270.

Lackland, D.T., T.J. Orchard, J.E. Keil, D.E. Saunders, F.C. Wheeler, L.J. Adams-Campbell, R.H. McDonald, and R.G. Knapp. 1992. Are race differences in the prevalence of hypertension explained by body mass and fat distribution? A survey in a biracial population. *International Journal of Epidemiology* 21(2):236-245.

Lewin-Epstein, N. 1991. Determinants of regular source of health care in black, Mexican, Puerto Rican, and non-Hispanic white populations. *Medical Care* 29(6):543-557.

Lurie, N., N.B. Ward, M.F. Shapiro, and R.H. Brook. 1984. Termination from Medi-Cal: Does it affect health? *New England Journal of Medicine* 314:1266-1268.

Ménard, J. 1989. Hypertension costs: Source, evolution and impact of cost-containment measures in various health-care systems. *Clinical and Experimental Hypertension-Theory and Practice*, A11(5,6):1149-1169.

Ostfeld, A.M., and E. Wilk. 1990. Epidemiology of stroke, 1980-1990: A progress report. *Epidemiologic Reviews* 12:253-256.

Patrick, D.L., C.W. Madden, P. Diehr, D.P. Martin, A. Cheadle, and S.M. Skillman. 1992. Health status and use of health services among families with and without health insurance. *Medical Care* 30:941-949.

Roccella, E.J., and M.J. Horan. 1988. The National High Blood Pressure Education Program: Measuring progress and assessing its impact. *Health Psychology* 7:(Suppl):297-303.

Rostand, S.G., K.A. Kirk, E.A. Rutsky, and B.A. Pate. 1982. Racial differences in the incidence of treatment for end-stage renal disease. *New England Journal of Medicine* 306:1276-1279.

Schneiderman, N. 1992. Ethnicity and ambulatory blood pressure measurement: Relationship to clinic and laboratory measurements. *Journal of Clinical Pharmacology* 32(7):604-609.

SHEP Cooperative Research Group. 1991. Prevention of stroke by antihypertensive drug treatment in older persons with isolated systolic hypertension: Final results of the systolic hypertension in the elderly program (SHEP). *Journal of the American Medical Association* 265:3255-3264.

Sorel, J.E., D.R. Ragland, and S.L. Syme. 1991. Blood pressure in Mexican Americans, Whites, and Blacks. *American Journal of Epidemiology* 134(4):370-378.

Stern, M.P., S.P. Gaskill, C.R. Allen, V. Garza, J.L. Gonzales, and R.H. Waldrop. 1981. Cardiovascular risk factors in Mexican Americans in Laredo, Texas, II: Prevalence and control of hypertension. *American Journal of Epidemiology* 113(5):556-562.

Svetkey, L.P., L.K. George, B.M. Burchett, P.A. Morgan, and D.G. Blazer. 1993. Black/white differences in hypertension in the elderly: An epidemiologic analysis in central North Carolina. *American Journal of Epidemiology* 137(1):64-73.

Temoshok, L., R.J. DiClemente, D.M. Sweet, M.S. Blois, and R.W. Sagbiel. 1984. Factors related to patient delay in seeking medical attention for cutaneous malignant melanoma. *Cancer* 54:3048-3053.

Thom, T.J., and J. Maurer. 1988. Time trends for coronary heart disease mortality and morbidity. In *Trends in Coronary Heart Disease Mortality: The Influence of Medical Care*, edited by M.W. Higgins and R.V. Luepker, 11. New York: Oxford University Press.

Treviño, F.M., and J.A. Moss. 1984. Health indicators for Hispanic, black and white Americans. *Vital and Health Statistics,* Series 10, Number 148. National Center for Health Statistics, DHHS pub. no. (PHS) 84-1576. Washington, DC: Government Printing Office.

Treviño, F.M., and J.A. Moss. 1983. Health insurance coverage and physician visits among Hispanic and non-Hispanic people. *Health— United States, 1983.* DHHS Pub. No. (PHS) 84-1232. Washington, DC: Government Printing Office.

Treviño, F.M., C.A. Stroup, and L. Ray. 1991. Health insurance coverage and utilization of health services by Mexican Americans, mainland Puerto Ricans, and Cuban Americans. *Journal of the American Medical Association* 265(2):233-237.

Valdez, R.B., H. Morgenstern, R. Brown, R. Wyn, C. Wang, and W. Cumberland. 1993. Insuring Latinos against the costs of illness. *Journal of the American Medical Association* 269(7):889-894.

Weissman, J.S., R. Stern, S.L. Fielding, and A.M. Epstein. 1991. Delayed access to health care: Risk factors, reasons, and consequences. *Annals of Internal Medicine* 114:325-331.

West, C. 1993. Reconceptualizing gender in physician-patient relationships. *Social Science Medicine* 36(1):57-66.

Wilcox, L.S., and W.D. Mosher. 1993. Factors associated with obtaining health screening among women of reproductive age. *Public Health Reports* 108(1):76-86.

Wolinsky, F.D., and R.J. Johnson. 1992. Perceived health status and mortality among older men and women. *Journal of Gerontology* 47(6):S304-S312.

Woodlander, S., and D.U. Himmelstein. 1988. Reverse targeting preventive care due to lack of insurance. *Journal of the American Medical Association* 259:2872-2874

Table 6.1
Sociodemographic data for individuals reporting hypertension by race/ethnicity, 1987

	WHITES	BLACKS	HISPANICS
GENDER *(percent)* A			
Male	50.73	38.24	40.31
Female	49.27	61.76	59.69
AGE *(mean number of years)* B	46.45	45.22	43.76
MARITAL STATUS *(percent)* A			
Never married	10.95	19.59	18.18
Married	73.46	45.48	60.40
Divorced	9.76	13.31	10.88
Separated	1.70	13.39	3.54
Widowed	4.14	8.24	7.00
EDUCATION *(mean number of years)* C	12.60	11.22	9.79
EDUCATION *(percent)* A			
None	1.10	1.68	3.46
1–8 years	7.55	15.67	34.38
9–11 years	13.37	27.27	18.24
12 years or more	77.98	55.38	43.92

SOURCE: 1987 National Medical Expenditure Survey
NOTE: Percents may not sum to 100 due to rounding.
A χ^2 statistic is significant at the level $p < 0.0001$.
B Analysis of variance (ANOVA) reveals significant differences between whites and Hispanics ($p < 0.01$).
C ANOVA reveals significant differences among categories ($p < 0.01$).

Table 6.2
Financial barriers A for individuals reporting hypertension by race/ethnicity, 1987
(In percents)

	WHITES	BLACKS	HISPANICS
UNEMPLOYED	30.37	44.63	45.76
AT/BELOW POVERTY	8.20	29.41	25.07
HEALTH INSURANCE COVERAGE B			
Private	73.82	50.90	47.18
Public	14.81	29.17	23.09
Uninsured	11.37	19.93	29.74

SOURCE: 1987 National Medical Expenditure Survey
A χ^2 statistic is significant for all three variables and categories at the level $p < 0.0001$.
B Percents may not sum to 100 due to rounding.

138

Table 6.3
Access barriers for individuals reporting hypertension by race/ethnicity, 1987
(In percents)

	WHITES	BLACKS	HISPANICS
HAVE USUAL SOURCE OF CARE A	87.38	84.05	74.97
TYPE OF USUAL CARE SOURCE B			
Doctor's office/group practice	77.16	62.82	61.85
Doctor's clinic	11.58	9.86	12.80
Neighborhood/family health center	1.96	7.09	11.29
Hospital outpatient clinic	4.03	13.55	7.71
Company/industrial clinic	0.70	0.46	0.41
School clinic	0.19	0.26	0.00
Hospital emergency room	0.90	2.96	3.10
Walk-in center	1.11	0.34	0.00
Patient's home	0.00	0.00	0.85
HMO	0.82	0.53	1.14
Other	1.53	2.12	0.84
TRANSPORTATION TO SOURCE OF CARE B			
Walking	3.19	6.10	5.95
Driving (self)	86.69	60.52	66.57
Being driven	8.25	20.71	16.95
Taxi	0.43	2.26	1.46
Other public transportation	1.03	9.25	9.08
Doctor usually comes to home	0.00	0.00	0.00
Other	0.41	1.16	0.00

SOURCE: 1987 National Medical Expenditure Survey
NOTE: Percents may not sum to 100 due to rounding.
A χ^2 statistic is significant at the level $p < 0.001$.
B χ^2 statistic is significant at the level $p < 0.0001$.

Table 6.4
Care received by individuals reporting hypertension by race/ethnicity, 1987

	WHITES	BLACKS	HISPANICS
Blood pressure checked last year *(percent)*	88.33	88.62	87.11
Mean number of doctor visits	4.53	4.06	3.76

SOURCE: 1987 National Medical Expenditure Survey
NOTE: Differences among categories for these variables are not statistically significant.

Table 6.5
Time barriers to care for individuals reporting hypertension by race/ethnicity, 1987

	WHITES	BLACKS	HISPANICS
Travel time to source *(minutes)*[A]	17.25	19.90	21.63
Time until appointment *(days)*	6.39	7.63	7.32
Time waiting in doctor's office *(minutes)*[A]	25.31	33.21	35.47

SOURCE: 1987 National Medical Expenditure Survey
[A] Analysis of variance (ANOVA) for travel time to source and time waiting in doctor's office reveals significant differences between whites and blacks and between whites and Hispanics ($p < 0.01$).

Table 6.6
Sociocultural barriers for individuals reporting hypertension by race/ethnicity, 1987
(In percents)

	WHITES	BLACKS	HISPANICS
PATIENT'S NATIVE LANGUAGE IS ENGLISH[A]	96.7	99.1	32.4
PATIENT FLUENT IN ENGLISH	96.5	79.3	60.4
(non-native English speakers) [B]	*N=68*	*N=6*	*N=185*
PHYSICIAN SPEAKS PATIENT'S NATIVE LANGUAGE [C]	100.0	NA	61.4
	N=1		*N=46*
PHYSICIAN'S RACE/ETHNICITY [A]			
American Indian	0.50	1.20	1.40
Alaska Native	0.03	0.38	0.00
Asian/Pacific Islander	6.04	5.60	13.86
Black	1.50	21.80	4.22
White	91.54	69.88	76.69
Puerto Rican (Hispanic)	0.37	1.14	3.84
PHYSICIAN'S GENDER *(percent male)*	94.07	90.51	90.75
MATCH BETWEEN PHYSICIAN AND PATIENT GENDER[A]	39.14	27.85	26.13

SOURCE: 1987 National Medical Expenditure Survey
[A] χ^2 statistic is significant at the level $p < 0.0001$. [B] χ^2 statistic is significant at the level $p < 0.001$.
[C] χ^2 statistic was not computed for this variable since more than one cell had fewer than five observations.

Table 6.7
Self-perception of health for individuals reporting hypertension by race/ethnicity, 1987
(In percents)

	WHITES	BLACKS	HISPANICS
Excellent	15.74	8.39	11.28
Good	56.62	44.87	43.54
Fair	22.14	36.35	35.91
Poor	5.50	10.39	9.27

SOURCE: 1987 National Medical Expenditure, Household Survey

NOTE: χ^2 statistic is significant at the level $p < 0.0001$; percents may not sum to 100 due to rounding.

CHAPTER 7

Racial and Ethnic Patterns of Hospital Emergency Room Use

Michael C. Thornton and Shelley I. White-Means

Although Americans generally have several health care options, most prefer having access to a private physician. However, for growing numbers of Americans, the emergency room (ER) has become a linchpin of medical care. This medical outlet began as a limited source of care for treating trauma and acute health conditions. Over time, its role has expanded, for many people supplanting the physician, outpatient facility, and clinic as their usual source of care (Torrens and Yedveb 1970; Aday, Fleming, and Andersen 1984). For them, it has become the so-called "community physician" (Satin and Duhl 1972). The reasons for this remain unclear, especially for racial/ethnic minorities who are most likely to use the ER in this way. To further our understanding of the factors that lead various groups to use the ER, we examined the association between a set of sociodemographic, structural, economic, and attitudinal variables and the use of ERs among African Americans, whites, and Hispanics.

LITERATURE REVIEW

Despite their growing popularity, ERs are generally considered an unattractive source of care. Services are usually discontinuous, which is associated with poorer health outcomes, and are obtained only after waiting long periods of time. For these and other reasons, patients are least satisfied with the treatment received at the ER although it remains one of the most expensive sources of medical care (Aday, Andersen, and Fleming 1980).

Nevertheless, certain qualities make the ER quite attractive. While outpatient facilities usually require an affiliation with a particular doctor, ERs do not. Individuals need not request an appointment to receive care, a requirement that makes the physician's office less desirable for some. In contrast to health clinics, the ER provides access to sophisticated medical technology. Finally, its hours of operation go beyond those of other health providers, and health insurance often covers its services.

While these qualities attract people of all races, other factors lead proportionately more racial/ethnic minorities to their doors. In fact, twice as many African Americans and Hispanics as whites report the ER as a source of care (Kasper and Garrish 1982). For African Americans and Hispanics, several sociohistorical factors typically are offered to explain the attraction to ERs: many hospitals are located in urban areas, close to inner-city neighborhoods, and have a tradition of free care; both groups tend not to have a regular doctor or health insurance as often as whites; both may be unaware of other health-care options; and many physicians in private practice have abandoned city-center environs for the suburbs (Bodenheimer 1970; Gold 1984; Gibson 1973; Neighbors 1986). That these groups continue to see the ER as a principal port of entry into the mainstream medical care system suggests that they have poor access to comprehensive health care and other sources of care (Aday, Fleming, and Andersen 1984; Dutton 1979; Guendelman and Schwalbe 1986; Sawyer 1982).

Cutting costs in this part of the medical care system has clear implications for the nature of care available in minority communities. Ignoring this reality and proceeding to cut rising medical care costs by focusing on the ER is disingenuous and may further close off options to minority populations. Before this course is taken, a better understanding of why racial/ethnic minorities make the medical choices they do is needed. It remains unclear what characteristics of users contribute to use of the ER and whether ER users understand their options.

Research has identified type of insurance, health status, employment status, age, and income as key to understanding use patterns of Medicaid recipients and those in poor health, two groups likely to use ER services (Stratmann and Ullman 1975). Per capita visits were negatively related to per capita income (Gold 1984). The most frequent users among black adults were the elderly, low-income persons, and the unemployed (Neighbors 1986). However, because this research does not distinguish between emergent and nonemergent visits to the ER, it is unclear which factors are associated with ER utilization when alternative health services are available.

Recent work has explored nonemergent use of medical facilities, including ERs. Regardless of other factors, African Americans are more likely than Hispanics to use ERs. White-Means, Thornton, and Yeo (1989) found that the poorest African Americans (versus middle-income respondents) and those who perceived themselves as in excellent (versus poor) health were most likely to go to ERs for nonemergent medical assistance. A good predictor of whether African Americans and Hispanics will choose the ER as the facility for nonemergent services is whether they view it as their usual source of care (White-Means and Thornton 1989).

Age and certain ailments are also associated with using the ER. Young adults are more likely than the oldest groups to use the ER. However, age and usage were not linearly related, since those who were 55 to 64 years of age chose it less often as than those who were older than 65 (White-Means and Thornton 1989). Finally, those who have digestive, impairment, and circulatory problems will more likely bring them to the ER than to other sources.

Left unanswered in previous research, primarily due to data limitations, is the role of cultural or attitudinal preferences in influencing patterns of ER use. Typically, research on use of medical care characterizes race/ethnicity as an intermediate factor for patterns of use. Presumably racial/ethnic heritage provides an indirect measure of group experience with aspects of life, including how one views health care. Inevitably, treating race/ethnicity as a proxy for perceptions about health care without exploring the influence of specific attitudes or cultural perceptions is problematic (White-Means and Thornton 1989). Clearly, racial/ethnic differences in trust in physicians, perceptions of the quality of care, and attitudes toward use of organized health-care delivery systems may account for disparate patterns of ER use. However, how do we know their influence without examining these attitudes specifically in statistical models? Few researchers have done this.

The analysis for this project makes two primary contributions to the literature on health services use. First, it adds to the work on nonemergent use of medical facilities. Data from a national survey are used to describe differences in the overall medical-use patterns of ER users and non-ER users among African Americans, whites, and Hispanics. Second, use of the ER and of other ambulatory medical facilities is predicted. The data source includes detailed information about attitudinal preferences for medical services, providing an opportunity to include new explanatory measures.

DATA

The data for this analysis are from the National Medical Expenditure Survey (NMES), 1987, conducted in rounds between Fall 1986 and Fall 1987 and sponsored by the Agency for Health Care Policy Research (Edwards and Berlin 1989; US DHHS 1992). (See Appendix.) The data represent the civilian, noninstitutionalized population of the United States via a sample of 36,000 respondents for whom health status, medical care expenditures, household composition, health insurance coverage, and other sociodemographics are provided. A subset of the primary NMES data file, including all Hispanic and non-Hispanic whites and African Americans who were between the ages of 21 and 65 in 1987, is used in this study.

The data source is ideal for the present analysis because it oversamples minorities, providing an opportunity to obtain a closer look at their circumstances. The data source is also unique in that it allows the researcher to append the primary sociodemographic and medical use data file with supplementary data files that contain information on factors frequently excluded from national data sources, such as diagnosed medical conditions and patients' attitudes about medical facilities.

Analysis Plan

The analysis plan for this study is twofold. First, descriptive data on patterns of ER use are examined according to race/ethnicity. These data on ER use are compared to data on use of other types of ambulatory services. Then use patterns are compared to those found in previous studies.

The second part of this analysis is an assessment of why persons visit the ER rather than another facility for nonemergent primary care. The NMES provides a detailed description of each respondent's ambulatory visits. For example, the data indicate whether a person visited the ER because a doctor told him to go there, whether the person was admitted to the hospital because of an ER visit, and whether the visit was for diagnosis or treatment, general checkup, maternity care, or immunizations. The factors associated with using the ER in cases where the visits meet three criteria are examined: not physician initiated, do not result in hospital stays, and do not entail surgical procedures; in essence, excluding ER visits that are true emergencies. While the three exclusionary criteria do not reveal all cases of persons with true emergencies, the data do not allow further sorting for emergent and nonemergent cases.

We use logistic regression analysis to contrast nonemergent ER use with use of outpatient facilities and other ambulatory medical provider visits. The sample includes persons with at least one ambulatory medical visit during the survey year, making it a user sample. The independent variables in the model are: (1) sociodemographic measures including age, education, marital status, and gender; (2) economic factors, including family income, employment status, family size, and health insurance; (3) structural factors including geographical location and having a usual source of care who is a physician; (4) potential cultural influences, including attitudes about health care and traditional medicine; and (5) a person's need, as measured by the presence of medical conditions that the World Health Organization groups in six major categories (digestive, impairments, circulatory, respiratory, arthritis, and all other conditions) (WHO 1975). In each part of this study, we perform the analyses separately, based on the respondent's race/ethnicity.

RESULTS

Table 7.1 reports average visits to medical facilities by those with at least one annual medical visit. These data are stratified according to whether or not the individual is a nonemergent ER user. The data indicate that African Americans and Hispanics are more likely than whites to visit the ER for nonemergent care. Additionally, among ER users, visits to this facility average 38.87 percent, 42.68 percent, and 34.21 percent of the annual medical visits made by Hispanics,

African Americans, and whites, respectively. Similarly, African Americans rely more heavily on outpatient departments for physician care than do either Hispanics or whites. Hispanic ER users have more visits to outpatient units than whites, although this relatively higher use does not occur among nonemergent ER users. The intermediate position for Hispanics may reflect a tendency to be more likely to use only the ER while whites are more likely to use both the ER and another ambulatory facility. As shown by "Other Ambulatory Providers Visits," both African Americans and Hispanics, when compared to whites, have low use of physician services in the provider's office. African Americans and Hispanics appear to compensate for low use of physician services in their offices by having high numbers of ER and outpatient facility visits.

The variables are defined in table 7.2; their means are presented in table 7.3. Table 7.4 reports the results of the logistic regression model of ER visits by race/ethnicity for the defined variables.

Findings by Variable Category

The consistent finding for all groups is that *medical need* is associated with use of the ER (table 7.4). Digestive and impairment conditions increase the likelihood of using the ER rather than another ambulatory facility for care by all groups. Respiratory conditions increase the likelihood of visits for African Americans and whites. Arthritis is associated with a greater chance of ER visits by whites.

When other variable classifications are considered, significant variations in ethnic/racial patterns of ER use emerge. Among whites only, variables in each of the five classifications of measures— sociodemographic, economic, structural, attitudinal, and need— influence use of the ER. Among Hispanics, attitudinal variables do not explain the choice to use the ER rather than another ambulatory facility. Among African Americans, economic variables do not provide clues about the relative use of the ER.

Hispanics, African Americans, and whites differ in the influence *sociodemographic* factors have on the choice of the ER as the ambulatory care facility. For Hispanics, marital status is a significant factor. Divorced or widowed Hispanics are more likely to use the ER than those who are married. Age is the sociodemographic variable of influence for African Americans. Older African Americans (but still under age 65) are less likely to use the ER. For whites, age, education, and marital status influence the use of the ER. Older, more educated, and never-married whites are least likely to use the ER. White males are more likely than white females to use the ER as their ambulatory care facility.

While *economic* factors are significant for Hispanics and whites, the specific variables of influence differ for the two groups.[1] Hispanics who have large families are more likely to use the ER. For whites, insurance status is the significant determinant of ER use. Whites with public health insurance are more likely than the uninsured to use the ER for nonemergent care.

Similarly, the role of *structural* factors differs for Hispanics and whites. Hispanics who reside in large SMSAs are less likely to use the ER than are those who reside outside these areas. For whites, those who do not live in SMSAs are more likely to use the ER.

Some *attitudes* are also important determinants of use of the ER for primary ambulatory care. If certain attitudes predispose one to use traditional sources of medical care, we would expect the use of the ER for nonemergent care to be limited. Since attitudes may vary by race/ethnicity, the influence of attitudes on use of the ER similarly may vary by race or ethnicity. African Americans who perceive that their own behavior determines recovery are less likely to use the ER. On the other hand, if African Americans perceive that getting medical services without cash is easy, they are more likely to visit the ER for care. Among whites, the perception that one's knowledge of health status is better than that of a physician is associated with a higher probability that the ER is chosen for primary care.

ER Users by Race/Ethnicity

A composite picture of an ER user does not exist. Lack of income or health insurance, traditional explanations for patterns of use, do not explain medical care choices fully. With the exception of some need variables, there is little overlap among the examined groups in the factors that determine visits. Thus, the particular qualities of each group should inform any policy.

For Hispanics, medical need and family situation best predict use of the ER. Difficulty with digestion, problems with blood and the nervous system, and impairments (i.e., disorders of the eye/ear, fractures, and sprains) significantly increase the chances that Hispanics will go to the ER. Persons suffering from these ailments may come to the ER because many of the associated conditions lend themselves to being treated in the ER. Sprains and fractures occur suddenly and often need immediate attention. Digestive disorders whose symptoms require prompt attention, make the ER a logical outlet for care. Hispanics who are separated from a spouse (divorced, separated, or widowed) and those from large families are also most likely to turn to the ER for medical assistance. Why disruption of marital status is an important predictor of ER use for Hispanics only is unclear.

Medical needs are clearly the most important predictors of whether African Americans will use the ER. Like Hispanics, digestive and impairment problems bring African Americans to ERs, as do diseases of the respiratory system. Apparently, certain ailments do not warrant ER care for certain populations. This pattern may be related to how much one believes that one's own behavior can help in recovery from a disease. While African Americans will bring particular ailments to ERs, they are less likely to go to these facilities if they also have a regular physician. Younger African Americans were more likely than their older counterparts to choose the ER over other options.

The three medical conditions found to be important predictors of ER use for African Americans also predict such behavior among whites. In addition, arthritis brings whites to ERs; only circulatory ailments do not bring them to ERs. That arthritis brings whites but not African Americans or Hispanics to ERs may reflect a difference in its prevalence in each community or in the levels of tolerance to it. Whites who do not live in SMSAs are more likely to use ERs. This relationship may reflect the influence that accessibility has on using these facilities. Whites' perceptions of whether they easily can obtain care without cash has no influence on service use. Whites with public health insurance also seem to target ERs for care. This is the only instance when a traditional economic factor is related to using ER services. Only one attitude was related to choice of medical care facility among whites: users who believed they knew their health better than their doctors were more likely to use the ER.

DISCUSSION

What do the data analyses suggest about factors that could deter use of the ER? As found in previous research, economic incentives such as income supplements or enhanced access to health insurance coverage will not lead African Americans and Hispanics, the heaviest ER users, to reduce their nonemergent visits to the ER and to present their medical conditions to other ambulatory facilities (White-Means and Thornton 1989). However, the data show that a usual source of care is central to curtailing ER use. How could we enhance access to a usual source of care? One way is to reduce the physical distance between the provider and recipient of care, thus minimizing the time and financial expenditures in getting to the source of care. Many recent state health reforms have tested another method of enhancing access—managed care. This type of provider coordination enables continuity of care, and thus could curtail ER use and channel patients to other ambulatory care providers.

Among African Americans, perceptions of being able to get care easily without cash increase the probability of using the ER rather than other ambulatory facilities for care. This finding suggests an additional method to curtail ER use. The ER may be overused because it is too easily accessible and perceived as a free service. One option to reduce use of ERs is requiring greater financial copayments by users of these facilities. Nevertheless, as a single approach, this could worsen access to facilities for those who use ERs when they have no other option.

When African Americans and Hispanics view other sources of medical care as viable alternatives, they will use these options and not ERs. For example, those who normally visit a private physician are much less likely to use the ER. While not true for other groups, for African Americans, curtailing the use of ERs must address the issue of how to make other medical options as attractive as the ER. If few alternatives are available, this complicates matters. Further, as long as many large urban hospitals make ER care readily accessible—patients do not need appointments, and charges for use of this facility are minimal—it will remain a popular source of care.

The type of illness and the stage at which patients come to the ER also may be key. Each group is more likely to bring certain ailments to this facility. Preventive measures targeting these diseases and encouraging earlier intervention would be in order. Emphasizing how one's own behavior is important to recovery, a belief significant among African Americans, might be a particular theme. However, changing the patterns for Hispanics is less clear. White-Means and Thornton (1995) found that despite relatively high annual expenditures, Hispanics make the smallest number of visits to ambulatory medical facilities. Thus, merely reducing the number of ER visits may not reduce annual expenditures. Emphasis must also be given to the stage of illness presented for treatment, a variable not included in the present data source and ignored in research on this population. Among Hispanics, special attention should be given to persons who live outside the 19 largest SMSAs and are members of large families.

The patterns described above do not resemble those for whites. While economic factors have been consistently unrelated to ER usage among racial/ethnic minorities, the same cannot be said for whites (White-Means and Thornton 1989). Whites with public, but not private, insurance were more likely to visit ERs. Thus, the only traditional economic influence on ER use is for whites, not African Americans or Hispanics.

One too easily might conclude that the limited number of significant attitudinal variables indicate that previous exclusions of such measures have been inconsequential. But care must be taken in coming to such a conclusion. The results indicate that within ethnic/racial groups, primarily Hispanics and to some extent whites, attitudes do not differ enough between ER and non-ER users to lead to distinct patterns of facility use. Nonetheless, differences in attitudes across racial/ethnic groups are significant. For example, NMES data indicate that 64 percent of white ER users perceive that their own behavior determines recovery, compared to 56 percent of Hispanics and 45 percent of African Americans (data not shown). Moreover, if the reported regression analysis were specified using racial/ethnic interaction terms, interactive effects on ER use would be found for the following attitudinal variables—*own behavior determines recovery, know health better than doctors,* and *get care easily without cash*. Thus, race/ethnicity interacts with attitudes to influence use or nonuse of the ER in nonemergent situations.

CONCLUSION

The characteristics of a typical ER user differ by race/ethnicity. Along with specific types of ailments, family status is an important determinant of use among Hispanics. For African Americans, having both a physician as a usual source of care and a set of beliefs about how much control they have in recovery play greater roles in choosing the ER. For African Americans and Hispanics, measured economic constructs have little effect. The qualities of typical white users of ERs are more likely to include economic factors (e.g., public vs. private insurance and employment status). There is no easy way to characterize the factors that bring these groups to ERs.

Further muddying the picture are two factors that are not captured by the available data. First, how the medical care landscape appears to the consumer cannot be measured. Do young black and Hispanic families go to ERs because they are unaware of other options in their communities, or because they know they have no other options? The present data do not provide an answer this question. The development of any policy to specify options should be contingent, of course, on providing an answer to this question. Second, perceptions of another sort were examined by the attitude variables. While examining these variables moves us closer to determining the importance of unique sets of attitudes that different groups bring to this issue, these measures remain inadequate in that they only indirectly get at cultural influences.

Attempting to rein in the cost of medical care is of course a complex effort. Yet, it often seems that policies attempting to do so assume that there is a homogeneous view of the medical care landscape. In this worldview, consumers have many options, but fail to avail themselves of some of them. Furthermore, these policies assume that the way to discourage inappropriate use of expensive facilities is via economic strategies that deny access without financial resources to pay for such care. As emerging work clearly indicates, these assumptions are, at best, too simplistic and, at worst, exacerbate a bad situation. Ignoring ethnic/racial differences compounds the problem. Once these differences are begun to be appreciated, policy can be created that will reflect the complex nature of today's society and the multidimensional aspects of American cultural life.

NOTES

1. Only among whites is ER use influenced by a traditional economic variable, i.e., having public health insurance. Having large families is classified as an economic variable in this analysis, although it is not a traditional one. Size of family correlates positively with demands on economic resources.

REFERENCES

Aday, L., R. Andersen, and G. Fleming. 1980. *Health Care in the United States: Equitable for Whom?* Beverly Hills, CA: Sage.

Aday, L., G. Fleming, and R. Andersen, 1984. *Access to Medical Care in the United States: Who Has It, Who Doesn't.* Chicago: Pluribus Press.

Bodenheimer, T. 1970. Patterns of American ambulatory care. *Inquiry* 7:26-37.

Dutton, D. 1979. Patterns of ambulatory health care in five different delivery systems. *Medical Care* 17:221-243.

Edwards, W.S., and M. Berlin. 1989. *Questionnaires and Data Collection Methods for the Household Survey and the Survey of American Indians and Alaska Natives.* National Medical Expenditure Survey: Method, No. 2. DHHS pub. no. (PHS) 89-3450. Rockville, MD: US Department of Health and Human Services, Public Health Service.

Gibson, G. 1973. Emergency medical services: A facet of ambulatory care. *Hospitals* 47:27-44.

Gold, M. 1984. The demand for hospital outpatient services. *Health Services Research* 19:383-412.

Guendelman, S., and J. Schwalbe. 1986. Medical care utilization by Hispanic children. *Medical Care* 24:925-937.

Kasper, J., and G. Garrish. 1982. *National Health Care Expenditures Study, Data Preview 12: Usual Sources of Medical Care and Their Characteristics.* DHHS pub. no. (PHS) 83-1572. Washington, DC: Government Printing Office.

Neighbors, H. 1986. Ambulatory medical care among adult black Americans: The hospital emergency room. *Journal of the National Medical Association* 78:275-282.

Satin, D., and F. Duhl. 1972. Help?—The hospital emergency unit as community physician. *Medical Care* 10:248-271.

Sawyer, D. 1982. Assessing access constraints on system equity: Source of care differences in the distribution of medical services. *Health Service Research* 17:27-44.

Stratmann, W., and R. Ullman. 1975. A study of consumer attitudes about health care: The role of the emergency room. *Medical Care* 13: 1033-1043.

Torrens, P., and D. Yedveb. 1970. Variations among emergency room populations: A comparison of four hospitals in New York City. *Medical Care* 13:1011-1020.

US Department of Health and Human Services (US DHHS), Agency for Health Care Policy and Research. 1992. *National Medical Expenditure Survey, 1987: Household Survey Population Characteristics and Person Level Utilization Rounds 1-4.* Rockville, MD: US DHHS.

White-Means, S., and M.C. Thornton. 1995. What cost savings could be realized by shifting patterns of use from hospital emergency rooms to primary care sites? *American Economic Review* 85(2):138-142.

White-Means, S., and M.C. Thornton. 1989. Nonemergent visits to hospital emergency rooms: A comparison of blacks and whites. *Milbank Quarterly* 67:35-57.

White-Means, S., M.C. Thornton, and J.S. Yeo. 1989. Sociodemographic and health factors influencing black and Hispanic use of the hospital emergency room. *Journal of the National Medical Association* 81:72-80.

World Health Organization (WHO). 1975. *Manual of the International Classification of Diseases, Injuries, and Causes of Death.* Based on the recommendation of the North Regional Conference, 1975, and adopted by the 29th Health Assembly. Geneva: WHO.

Table 7.1

Medical utilization patterns by use of the emergency room and race/ethnicity, 1987

	WHITES		BLACKS		HISPANICS	
	ER N=1,050	non-ER N=7,821	ER N=550	non-ER N=1,975	ER N=143	non-ER N=1,058
Percent of all medical visits made to emergency room	34.21	0.00	42.68	0.00	38.87	0.00
Average number of emergency room visits	1.30	0.00	1.57	0.00	1.33	0.00
Average number of outpatient unit visits	1.23	0.67	1.45	1.15	1.34	0.44
Average number of other ambulatory providers visits	7.44	6.65	5.68	4.87	5.73	5.27

SOURCE: 1987 National Medical Expenditure Survey

NOTE: The category "ER" indicates persons with at least one nonemergent ER visit during the year. "Non-ER" indicates persons with at least one ambulatory medical visit during the year but no nonemergent ER visits (i.e., all visits were to outpatient units or other ambulatory provider facilities).

Table 7.2
Variable measures for logistic regressions

VARIABLES	DESCRIPTION
SOCIODEMOGRAPHIC	
Age	In years
Education	Years of formal education
Never married	= 1 if never married; 0 otherwise
Widowed	= 1 if widowed; 0 otherwise
Divorced/separated	= 1 if divorced or separated; 0 otherwise
Sex	= 1 if male; 0 otherwise
ECONOMIC	
Family income	In dollars
Family size	= 1 if two or more persons in family; 0 otherwise
Public health insurance	= 1 if Medicaid, Medicare, CHAMPUS, or other public insurance; 0 otherwise
Private health insurance	= 1 if health insurance through a private source; 0 otherwise
STRUCTURAL	
Employed	= 1 if employed; 0 otherwise
Nonsouth region	= 1 if live outside the South; 0 otherwise
Largest SMSAs	= 1 if live in one the 19 largest SMSAs; 0 otherwise
Non-SMSA	= 1 if does not live in a SMSA; 0 otherwise
Usual source of care is physician	= 1 if usual source of care is a physician; 0 otherwise
ATTITUDINAL	
Can get well without doctor	= 1 if perceive can get well without doctor; 0 otherwise
Home remedies are better	= 1 if perceive home remedies are better than prescription medicine; 0 otherwise
Own behavior determines recovery	= 1 if perceive own behavior determines recovery; 0 otherwise
Know health better than doctor	= 1 if perceive know health better than doctor; 0 otherwise
Get care easily without cash	= 1 if perceive can get care easily without cash; 0 otherwise
Luck big part of recovery	= 1 if perceive luck is a big part of recovery; 0 otherwise
NEED	
Digestive	= 1 if have medical visits due to disease of the digestive, blood, and nervous system; 0 otherwise

Continued on next page

Table 7.2 continued

VARIABLES	DESCRIPTION
Impairment	= 1 if have medical visits due to impairments, including disorders of the eye and ear, fractures and sprains; 0 otherwise
Circulatory	= 1 if have medical visits due to hypertension, heart disease, or other circulatory problems; 0 otherwise
Respiratory	= 1 if have medical visits due to diseases of the respiratory system; 0 otherwise
Arthritis	= 1 if have diseases of the musculoskeletal system and connecting tissues; 0 otherwise

SOURCE: 1987 National Medical Expenditure Survey

Table 7.3
Means of variable measures for logistic regressions according to race/ethnicity

	WHITES *N*=7,838	BLACKS *N*=1,912	HISPANICS *N*=927
SOCIODEMOGRAPHIC			
Age	40.40	39.10	38.10
Education	13.10	11.90	10.60
Married	0.69	0.42	0.62
Sex	0.44	0.38	0.41
ECONOMIC			
Family income	41,640	26,164	28,752
Family size	0.83	0.79	0.86
Public health insurance	0.11	0.28	0.18
Private health insurance	0.85	0.59	0.60
STRUCTURAL			
Employed	0.76	0.64	0.69
Nonsouth region	0.69	0.44	0.67
Largest SMSAs	0.25	0.37	0.38
Non-SMSA	0.25	0.21	0.19
Usual source of care is physician	0.62	0.49	0.46
ATTITUDES			
Can get well without doctor	0.54	0.39	0.40
Home remedies are better	0.24	0.29	0.28
Behavior determines recovery	0.65	0.52	0.52
Know health better than doctor	0.42	0.39	0.36
Luck big part of recovery	0.07	0.13	0.11
Get care easily without cash	0.22	0.21	0.25
NEED			
Digestive	0.11	0.13	0.11
Impairment	0.22	0.16	0.16
Circulatory	0.13	0.20	0.11
Respiratory	0.26	0.20	0.22
Arthritis	0.15	0.14	0.13

SOURCE: 1987 National Medical Expenditure Survey

Table 7.4
Logistic regression of emergency room use, according to race/ethnicity

	WHITES N=7,838	BLACKS N=1,912	HISPANICS N=927
SOCIODEMOGRAPHIC			
Age A	-0.038***	-0.017**	-0.015
Education	-0.104***	-0.036	0.007
Marital status			
Never married	-0.283**	-0.067	-0.316
Divorced/separated	0.195	-0.185	0.612**
Widowed	0.085	-0.236	1.505***
Married	Reference group	Reference group	Reference group
GENDER			
Male	0.307***	0.001	-0.004
Female	Reference group	Reference group	Reference group
ECONOMIC			
Family income A	-1.10E-06	-3.32E-06	1.75E-06
FAMILY SIZE			
Two or more	-0.085	-0.009	0.956**
Less than two	Reference group	Reference group	Reference group
INSURANCE STATUS			
Public insurance	0.348***	0.223	-0.112
Private insurance	-0.155	-0.208	-0.208
Uninsured	Reference group	Reference group	Reference group
STRUCTURAL			
Employment status			
Employed	-0.171*	0.143	0.157
Unemployed	Reference group	Reference group	Reference group
Region of residence			
Nonsouth region	0.059	-0.073	0.135
South	Reference group	Reference group	Reference group

Continued on next page

Table 7.4 continued

	WHITES N=7,838	BLACKS N=1,912	HISPANICS N=927
Area of residence			
Largest SMSAs	0.036	-0.010	-0.404*
Non-SMSA	0.153*	-0.108	-0.250
Small SMSAs	Reference group	Reference group	Reference group
Regular provider			
Usual source of care is physician	-0.049	-0.427***	-0.348*
Usual source of care is not physician	Reference group	Reference group	Reference group
ATTITUDES B			
Can get well without doctor	-0.019	-0.007	-0.103
Home remedies are better	-0.108	0.104	0.210
Own behavior determines recovery	-0.077	-0.292**	-0.131
Know health better than doctors	0.140*	-0.133	0.357
Get care easily without cash	0.052	0.257*	-0.235
Luck big part of recovery	0.208	-0.074	0.302
NEED C			
Digestive	0.558***	0.970***	1.238***
Impairment	0.940***	0.886***	1.290***
Circulatory	0.081	0.125	0.017
Respiratory	0.337***	0.521***	0.311
Arthritis	0.429***	0.269	-0.045
All other conditions	Reference group	Reference group	Reference group
SUMMARY STATISTICS			
Percent ER user	11.15	20.61	13.27
-2 Log likelihood	5148.49	1804.96	659.84
χ^2	447.96***	140.30***	65.93***

SOURCE: 1987 National Medical Expenditure Survey
A Continuous variable
B Dichotomous variable
C The six groups are digestive, impairments, circulatory, respiratory, arthritis, and all other conditions.
* $p > 0.10$ ** $p > 0.05$ *** $p > 0.01$

Re-examining Federal and State Roles in Assuring Equitable Access to Health Care

Marsha D. Lillie-Blanton and Charisse Lillie[1]

Assuring access to health care historically has been considered the domain of state and local governments. Nonetheless, the federal government, during the last half of the twentieth century, used a combination of statutory, regulatory, and financing strategies to expand access and reduce discriminatory practices in the health marketplace. The unprecedented growth in federal health expenditures, however, has resulted in renewed interest in limiting federal involvement in health. It is, therefore, no surprise that several of the recently debated national health reform proposals have aimed at expanding the role of states in organizing systems of health-care financing and delivery. From the federal government's perspective, the proposals had as their implicit, if not explicit, goal to minimize increases in federal health expenditures. From the perspective of state governments, they provided a means to limit unfunded federal mandates while allowing states to decide how best to meet the health needs of their residents.

Many states devote a considerable share of their budgets to health and are currently taking a leadership role in developing innovative approaches to reducing barriers to care (Altman and Morgan 1983; National Association of State Budget Officers 1994; Toiv, Schuyler, and Roskin 1992; Lipson 1994). However, tension among federal, state, and local policymakers has increased as governors and mayors attempt to respond to unfunded federal health-care mandates. As federal resources to support state health-care needs decline, it is not readily apparent whether vulnerable populations would fare better or worse with increased state responsibility for health. Hispanics and

African Americans have had varying experiences with state governments over controversial issues such as voting rights, desegregation of schools, and the rights of immigrants. In many states, disagreements were resolved only as a consequence of federal legislation or federal court decisions. In light of ongoing efforts to strengthen the role of states in organizing systems of health financing and services delivery, this study examines the impact of the current division of governmental responsibility on Hispanics' and African Americans' access to care.

SCOPE OF THE INVESTIGATION

As policymakers continue the debate on how to reform the U.S. health-care system, defining appropriate federal and state governmental roles in reducing barriers in access to care remains one of many contentious issues. This study seeks to provide insight into the likely outcomes of health reforms that would reduce the federal presence in health and strengthen the role of states. The study uses a framework rooted in two disciplinary fields—law and public health—to examine the impact of the current division of governmental efforts. Since both disciplines have been involved in efforts to remedy inequalities in health care, a cross-disciplinary assessment should be beneficial because it pulls together knowledge gained from both perspectives.

This study has three primary objectives: (1) to identify constitutional/ statutory provisions that guide federal/state governmental roles in assuring equitable access to care; (2) to examine what is known about the effectiveness of governmental provisions in reducing barriers to care facing racial/ethnic minority populations; and (3) to assess, using a national data source, the impact of the provisions on minority populations' access to care within and across geographic regions of the United States.

Methods

The investigation used qualitative and quantitative research methods. To identify constitutional or statutory provisions that guide federal and state roles in health, legal and historical research methods were used. To examine the adequacy of these provisions and their impact on access, this study analyzed information from a combination of sources including case law, constitutional principles, and studies and reports evaluating various aspects of the provisions. Additionally, data from the 1987 National Medical Expenditure Survey (NMES) were analyzed to assess differences in indicators of potential and realized access to care. (See Appendix.)

Access indicators were compared for poor and near-poor Hispanics, African Americans, and whites within and across the four U.S. geographic regions defined by the U.S. Census Bureau—the Northeast, Midwest, South, and West (figure 8.1). Unless otherwise noted, population group estimates are identified as different only if the 95 percent confidence intervals do not overlap. The assessment focused on poor and near-poor Americans (defined as individuals with incomes below 200 percent of the federal poverty level) because this is the subgroup of the population most likely to need government resources to gain access to care. Although there are limitations in using regional data to make inferences about the practices of state governments, these data are the best available proxy indicators for the experiences of populations within and across state boundaries.

Figure 8.1
U.S. regions, 1994

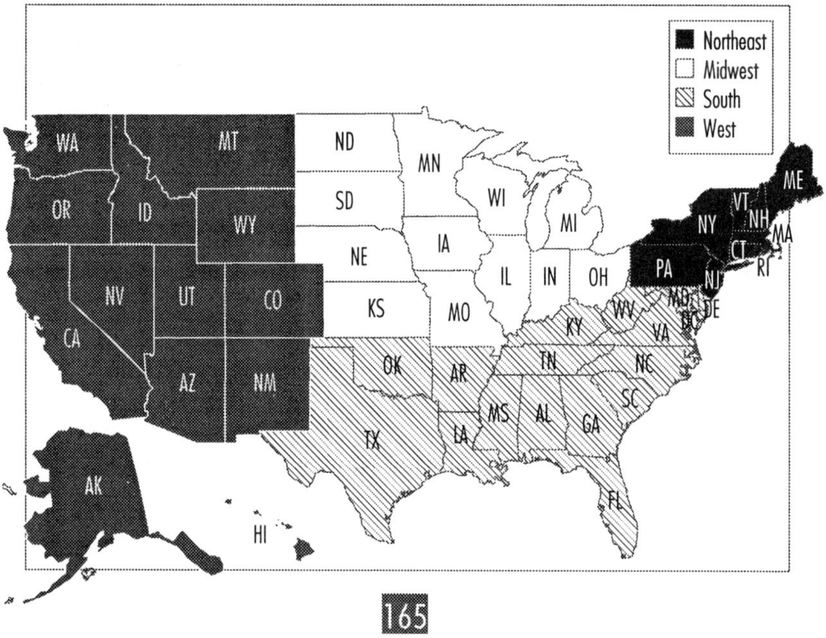

LEGAL BASIS FOR DIVISION OF RESPONSIBILITY FOR HEALTH

While it is apparent that the United States Constitution—principally the Tenth Amendment—delegates responsibility for domestic affairs to the states, it is equally clear that the federal government has authority under current interpretations of the Constitution to assume responsibility for public health. The Tenth Amendment reserves those powers neither granted to Congress, nor denied to the states, to the states and the people. Thus, each state retains primary control over local concerns. Nonetheless, Congress derives authority for federal legislation in health-care financing and delivery from constitutional provisions that grant it powers to tax and spend "for the general welfare" and powers in matters of "national interests."

In the earliest days of this nation, it was understood that health laws fell within the "police powers" of the state, defined as their authority to provide for the general health, safety, and welfare of citizens (Gibbons v. Ogden, 22 U.S., Wheaton, 1, 89, 1824).[2] The concept of the "general welfare" was circumscribed by the Tenth Amendment's principle of state autonomy.

Two court cases give evidence of the authority of states. In 1922, the Supreme Court ruled the Child Labor Tax Law to be "an illicit attempt by Congress to regulate the exclusive state power over the employment of child labor" (Bailey v. Drexel Furniture Co., Child Labor Tax Case, 259 U.S. 20, 1922). Similarly, the Court invalidated the Agricultural Adjustment Act of 1933, characterizing the plan as an attempt "to purchase a compliance which the Congress is powerless to command" (United States v. Butler, 297 U.S. 1, 1936). The plan attempted to raise farm prices by reducing production.

Using the design of the framers of the Constitution, the federal government is a government of limited powers, which can be exercised only in matters of national interest. National interests, historically, were considered international affairs (e.g., defense) and interstate issues (e.g., commerce). Local interests, historically, were almost synonymous with domestic issues.

A blurring of the distinctions between local and national interests occurred during the Great Depression when social issues were defined as matters of national interest. The New Deal legislation of the 1930s redefined the role of the federal government in providing for the general welfare. It was during this period that the Social Security Act was passed, providing retirement pensions and unemployment compensation on a national basis. Both provisions were upheld by the Supreme Court as legitimate exercises of Congressional power to tax and spend for the general welfare (Helvering v. Davis, 301 U.S. 619, 1937; Steward Machine Co. v. Davis, 301 U.S. 548, 1937). These 1937 Supreme Court rulings established precedent for domestic issues to be interpreted as national interests.

Thus, evolving concepts of local and national interests have unquestionably established a federal role in health-care financing and delivery. With the Great Society programs of the 1960s, an evolved definition of national interests had become fairly entrenched in the minds of the public, if not in the minds of legislators. After a fiercely fought battle among legislators, the Congress succeeded in using its authority to tax and spend for the general welfare as the basis for creating Medicare in 1965, a totally federal program, and Medicaid, a federal-state health-care financing program.

Currently espoused views that seek to limit federal responsibility in health are a result of strict interpretations of constitutional limits on federal power. This dichotomy between "strict" and "broad" constitutional interpretations sets up a tension in the political arena reflected in the 1990's debate on health-care reform. Many believe that the interpretation of domestic issues as national interests has gone beyond constitutional limits on federal power. However, as Justice Sandra Day O'Connor succinctly explained:

> The framework [of the Constitution] has been sufficiently flexible over the past two centuries to allow for enormous changes in the nature of government. The federal government undertakes activities today that would have been unimaginable to the framers in two senses; first, because the framers would not have conceived that *any* government would conduct such activities; and second, because the framers would not have believed that the *federal* government, rather than the states, would assume such responsibilities. (New York v. United States, 112 S.Ct. 2408, 2418 [1992])

In sum, the Constitution may serve as the framework, but it does not define the outer limits of what can be done at each level of govern-

ment. It is the responsibility of the legislative branch of government
to define those outer limits.

ARE CURRENT PROVISIONS ADEQUATE TO ASSURE EQUITABLE ACCESS IN PRINCIPLE?

Tables 8.1 and 8.2 identify currently operative, key governmental
provisions that are intended to reduce barriers to care. Most of the
provisions were not specifically designed to address the needs of
minority populations, but target characteristics, such as lack of
income, that increase a population's vulnerability, irrespective of
race/ethnicity. The effectiveness of these provisions—particularly
Medicaid and Medicare—in reducing barriers to care has been
documented in numerous studies (Newacheck 1988; O'Brian,
Rodgers and Baugh 1985; Link, Long, and Settle 1982). Of concern is
whether the existing provisions are sufficient given the nature of
problems that persist today. Thus, this assessment examines current
indicators of the provisions' effectiveness.

Federal Government Provisions

As noted in table 8.1, the federal government has used a combination of approaches to improve access to health care. Contrasting
measures of health and health-care use prior to and after enactment
of these provisions gives evidence of improved access (Davis et al.
1989). Indications of improvements are particularly significant given
that many health status measures showed minimal or no change in
the years preceding the federal government's major involvement in
the financing and delivery of health services. Prior to 1965, for
example, the use of physician and hospital services differed dramati-
cally by race and income. However, between 1965 and 1980, racial
differences in the use of health services narrowed considerably. The
record of accomplishment is remarkable. Several issues of concern,
however, deserve note, including the monitoring and enforcement of
antidiscriminatory provisions, the evaluation of initiatives that sought
to develop health resources for underserved populations, and the
intersection of racial and economic discriminatory practices.

Monitoring and enforcement of antidiscriminatory provisions.
Several federal laws e.g., the Hill Burton Act, Title VI of the Civil
Rights Act, prohibit discrimination by providers who receive federal

funds or offer services to the public. The federal government, however, has failed in recent years to monitor or enforce these provisions actively within the health-care sector. Since discriminatory practices are now less overt and sometimes unintentional (e.g., practice location decisions, the selective granting of hospital admitting privileges), the lack of aggressive oversight allows providers failing to comply with the law to go undetected.

The Hill Burton Act of 1946 was one of the earliest legislative provisions that prohibited discrimination and, thus, played an early role in expanding access to care for poor and racial minority Americans.[3] In 1975, the Congress authorized a new Hill-Burton program that reflected its concern with the noncompliance levels and lack of enforcement effort under the old program. Until 1972, the regulations implementing the Hill-Burton uncompensated care obligation simply tracked the language of the statute in requiring a facility to provide a "reasonable volume" of free care. From 1972 until 1979, a facility could comply with its obligation by either providing a minimum percentage of uncompensated care or by maintaining an "open door policy." The new regulations, issued in 1979, set more stringent standards for compliance and a clear definition of reasonable volume (Armstrong v. Fairmont Community Hospital Association, Inc., 659 F.Supp. 1524, 1532-33, D. Minn., 1987). To comply with the law, the new standards required a Hill-Burton facility to provide each year, for a period of twenty years, uncompensated services at a level not less than the lesser of 3 percent of its operating costs or 10 percent of the amount of federal assistance (42 C.F.R. 124.501, 124.503). However, by the mid-1980s, the new regulations were less effective in reducing barriers to care because many hospitals had completed their twenty-year obligations or were already providing more than 3 percent of their operating costs in uncompensated care.

Title VI of the Civil Rights Act of 1964 hastened the process of desegregation in health facilities. By prohibiting racial discrimination by recipients of federal funds, the provision helped to bring to an end policies and practices that excluded minority populations from services. The Office of Civil Rights (OCR) of the Department of Health and Human Services (formerly the Department of Health, Education, and Welfare) has primary responsibility for enforcement of Title VI.

Enforcement mechanisms include: (1) requiring assurances from Medicare/Medicaid certified facilities, (2) requiring state agencies to submit compliance plans for state enforcement activities, (3) investigating accusations of noncompliance, and (4) conducting studies.

In 1980, the director of OCR acknowledged that its record in combatting discrimination in health care was bleak in comparison to its achievements in education (U.S. Commission on Civil Rights 1980). Concerns about the adequacy of enforcement provisions resulted in a lawsuit, filed just before the end of the Bush Administration. The suit alleged that OCR had abdicated its Title VI enforcement responsibilities by failing to compile and analyze the data necessary for effective enforcement in health care (Madison-Hughes v. Shalala, Civ. No. 393-0048).[4] Plaintiffs' counsel has been in negotiations with the Clinton Administration regarding settlement of the suit.

Health resources. Since 1963, at least 40 programs, established under Titles VII and VIII of the Public Health Service Act, have been developed to influence the supply of health providers in medically underserved communities (table 8.1). The General Accounting Office concluded that evaluations conducted to date of 30 Title VII and VIII programs have failed to demonstrate a significant effect on the supply, distribution, and representation of minority health professionals (Baumgartner et al. 1994). Based on this finding, however, it would be premature to conclude that these programs have been ineffective, since many of the programs were not organized to systematically generate the type of information needed for an evaluation of outcome.

For example, since 1960 there have been numerical and proportionate increases in minority health providers; however, neither the increase in supply nor the program incentives have been adequate to reduce substantially the maldistribution of health resources (Lewin and Rice 1994). The extent to which either the increase in supply or the maldistribution can be attributed to government policies cannot be determined from the available data. It is the failure to recognize the importance of collecting outcome data and of evaluating program impact that now results in a superficial understanding of the effectiveness of past efforts and in conclusions that suggest that government policies were misguided.

Intersection of racial and economic discrimination. Of particular concern is that the combination of racial and economic discriminatory practices are not within the purview of civil rights laws. Civil rights laws only give cause of action for what are defined as immutable characteristics. Thus, poor and near-poor Americans are not a protected class. Protected classes include, for example, those defined by race, gender, age, or national origin. Current law, therefore, permits a health facility, with the exception of emergency care, to deny services to persons unable to pay. Since Hispanics and African Americans are disproportionately poor or near-poor, many are doubly at risk of encountering barriers in the health marketplace.

State and Local Government Provisions

Several of the state governmental efforts to reduce barriers in access to care mirror those at the federal level (table 8.2). However, consistent with historical interpretations of state authority, state governments perform a more extensive role in health. In addition to financing programs, states provide health services for medically indigent populations and have regulatory authority over the insurance industry. State provisions designed to reduce barriers in access to care have faced a myriad of challenges, particularly as federal dollars to support these initiatives have declined and health costs have continued to rise. Several of the issues of concern include Medicaid eligibility and payment rates, the existing recourse when services are inadequate, oversight of the insurance industry, and enforcement of the Fourteenth Amendment.

Medicaid eligibility and payment rates. As a combined federal/ state program, Medicaid allows states broad discretion in defining eligibility within federal guidelines. By federal law, a state's Medicaid program must extend eligibility to certain classes of the poor, generally referred to as the "categorically needy." The categorically needy includes individuals eligible for assistance under the Aid to Families with Dependent Children (AFDC) Program and the aged, blind, and totally disabled, who are entitled to receive assistance under the federal Supplemental Security Income (SSI) Program. States vary considerably, however, in the income guidelines used to determine who qualifies as categorically needy. Also, states vary in budgetary resources and philosophical views about funding of services for low-income populations.

Loprest and Gates (1993) estimated that as of 1990, Medicaid, on average, enrolled about half of the nonelderly poor population in the nation. As shown in table 8.3, the percentage enrolled varies by region. Medicaid covered nearly 60 percent of the poor in the Middle Atlantic states (New Jersey, New York, Pennsylvania), the New England states (Connecticut, Maine, Massachusetts, New Hampshire, Rhode Island, Vermont), and the East North Central states (Illinois, Iowa, Michigan, Ohio, Wisconsin). In contrast, Medicaid covered less than 40 percent of the poor in the Mountain states (Arizona, Colorado, Idaho, Montana, Nevada, New Mexico, Utah, Wyoming) and the West South Central states (Arkansas, Louisiana, Oklahoma, Texas).

Differences in the extent of Medicaid coverage, in part, are a consequence of many factors, including the variability among states in outreach to eligible beneficiaries. Another factor, however, that accounts for the variability is the linkage of Medicaid with income assistance programs that also have eligibility rules that vary from state to state. Due to the fiscal problems facing many state governments, this linkage is a disincentive to expand Medicaid eligibility. Recent changes in federal law have severed some of the linkage to income assistance programs by promulgating federal definitions of Medicaid eligibility that supersede more limited state rules (Rowland, Feder, and Salganicoff 1993). The Omnibus Budget Reconciliation Act of 1989 (P.L.101-239) requires states to cover pregnant women, infants, and children through age five whose family incomes do not exceed 133 percent of the federal poverty level, and children over age six born after September 30, 1983, whose families' income does not exceed the federal poverty level. Nonetheless, many poor two-parent families and families without young children are excluded from Medicaid because of categorical eligibility rules.

Medicaid's lower payment rates for physicians affect their willingness to provide services to Medicaid beneficiaries. A secondary negative effect is on the growth of the health services delivery infrastructure in minority communities. Medicaid rates are lower than private fees in every state (Loprest and Gates 1993), paying, on average, about 60 percent of the amount paid by private payers (table 8.3). Medicaid payment rates, in relation to private rates, are highest in the West South Central states (Arkansas, Louisiana, Oklahoma,

Texas) and lowest in the Middle Atlantic states (New Jersey, New York, Pennsylvania). Thus, while Medicaid coverage of the poor is higher in the Middle Atlantic states than in other parts of the United States, payment rates are lower. Coverage rates in the Pacific states (Alaska, California, Hawaii, Oregon, Washington) of the West, the region with the largest share and number of Hispanics, are higher than average, but payment rates are lower. Conversely, the largest share of African Americans resides in the South, a region with higher payment rates on average but with lower coverage rates than in other parts of the United States. The consequences of these divergent patterns for access will depend on factors such as the availability of publicly supported health-care resources and the willingness of private providers to care for uninsured and underinsured residents.

Recourse for inadequate services. Many Hispanics and African Americans use publicly funded health services due, in part, to higher rates of uninsured persons and to the lack of private providers in minority communities. Across the country, publicly financed or supported health facilities generally are underfunded, understaffed, and physically unappealing, although the extent of these problems varies. In some respects, they could be described as "separate and unequal" health-care resources. Yet, in underserved communities, they may be the only health resource and, therefore, invaluable. Of concern is that states generally cannot be held legally responsible for the amount or quality of services provided in public health facilities. Only when federal or state law imposes a mandatory duty to provide care for the poor is there recourse. Legal actions can be brought to remedy a state's failure to fund a medical assistance program adequately. Courts in California and New York, for example, have held that a county cannot avoid a mandatory duty to provide relief to the poor because of lack of funding.

However, in many states, the provision of health care to low-income populations is merely authorized, not mandated. State authority does not mean that adequate funding will be appropriated. Thus, declining revenues and limited funds are often sufficient cause to terminate or reduce funding for services. Furthermore, the amount available to spend on services for the medically indigent may be limited. Most counties fund their medical assistance programs through property taxes, and many states have statutorily limited the rates that can be levied for property taxes. Other states have explicitly limited the amount that can be expended on indigent care. Therefore, some courts have held that a county cannot be held liable for indigent medical care beyond its available budget (Dowell 1989).

States also provide health care for medically indigent populations through public hospitals. In recent years, an increasing number of public and private hospitals have faced financial difficulties, resulting in their sale, closure, or merger. Although one study found that public hospitals are less likely to close than their private nonprofit or for-profit counterparts, the consequences of a public hospital's closure may be greater because it provides services to clients for whom there is little competition in the private sector (Lillie-Blanton et al. 1992). Attempts to prevent the closure of public hospitals have met with limited success. For example, the Commonwealth Court of Pennsylvania refused to enjoin the closing of Philadelphia General Hospital. The court rejected the argument that a two-hundred-year history of statutes authorizing a hospital for the indigent in Philadelphia required the city to maintain Philadelphia General Hospital as such (Preston v. City of Philadelphia).

Oversight of insurance industry. State regulatory authority of the insurance industry is important for several reasons. States protect consumers in the private health insurance market through functions such as licensing and monitoring the solvency of insurers, approving premium rates, and investigating complaints regarding unfair business practices. Since 1975, however, state oversight of the health insurance industry has been declining. GAO estimates that only about one-fourth of the nation's health expenditures are currently paid by private insurance that is regulated by state insurance departments (Alcocer, Rasmussen, and Forland 1994). The remaining health-care expenditures are paid through two sources: (a) 34 percent are paid by employer plans or out-of-pocket by individuals and (b) 42 percent is paid by government health programs such as Medicaid and Medicare. Employers, especially large companies, are increasingly choosing to self-insure their employees. These employers are preempted from state regulation by a provision of the federal Employee Retirement Income Security Act (ERISA).[5] The ERISA preemption is a major hurdle for states attempting health insurance reform. In effect, it limits state regulatory powers to only the insurance industry since states do not have authority to regulate employer self-insured health plans.

As a consequence of the increasing number of employer self-insured health plans, states are less able to protect consumers in the private insurance market. For low-income Americans with private coverage, state oversight could be critical in efforts to maintain and improve access to care. Private health coverage was reported by an estimated 26 percent of low-income Hispanics, 27 percent of low-income African Americans, and 49 percent of low-income whites, according to analysis of the NMES data (figure 8.2). Hispanics and African Americans are more likely than whites to be employed in service occupations and in positions classified as operators or fabricators

Figure 8.2

Percent of poor/near-poor persons by health insurance status, 1987

Persons under age 65

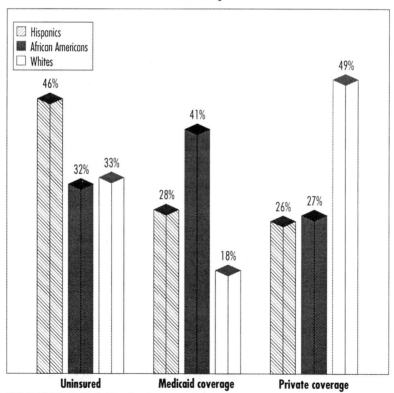

SOURCE: 1987 National Medical Expenditure Survey

175

(US Bureau of the Census 1991). These are positions in which not only is the compensation less but protections also are fewer than in managerial, professional, or technical positions. Thus, the scope of benefits of the plans, the required deductibles, and copayments of these plans may well determine whether certain types of care are accessible and to what extent. For low- and moderate-income families, the cost-sharing provisions of an insurance plan are critical.

The Fourteenth Amendment. The equal protection clause of the Fourteenth Amendment to the U.S. Constitution requires that states treat similarly situated persons similarly. If a state law discriminates on the basis of a "suspect" classification (race, national origin, or alienage) or in the exercise of a fundamental right, a court will apply strict scrutiny, which requires such a law to be struck down unless the government can show that the law is necessary to achieve a compelling state interest (Lockhart et al. 1986). For example, denying benefits to lawfully resident immigrants would be subject to strict scrutiny.

However, even individuals who are members of protected classes may face barriers related to racial/ethnic origin. Children of undocumented immigrants who are born in the United States, for example, are a protected class because they are U.S. citizens. Nonetheless, some parents may not seek care for an eligible child because of concern about their own status; others may seek care, but are placed in a situation of falsifying information to gain some level of access. More-over, some providers collect and report information on the immigration status of patients—a practice that may deter use of services by parents who fear that their status may be revealed to authorities. For example, although undocumented pregnant women in California were eligible for prenatal care under MediCal, several providers reported that the women would discontinue care when asked to submit an application for MediCal benefits (Arnold et al. 1994).

Although persons who suspect they are facing discrimination can seek recourse through the courts, legal suits are relatively few. This could be related to the lack of financial means or the lack of information about how to file such claims. Organizations such as the NAACP Legal Defense Fund, the National Council of LaRaza, the National Health Law Project, and state-based Legal Services Corporations provide a legal safety net for the filing of individual or class-action suits by those asserting claims of discrimination. However, proving discrimination is difficult because constitutional violations require proof of intent, a standard that is higher than for other types of claims.

RACIAL/ETHNIC DIFFERENCES IN ACCESS TO CARE WITHIN AND ACROSS U.S. GEOGRAPHIC REGIONS

Of the 204 million white, Hispanic, and African Americans under 65 years of age in 1987, 78 percent are non-Hispanic white, 13 percent are non-Hispanic black, and 9 percent are Hispanic. In contrast to whites, Hispanics and African Americans are geographically concentrated within several regions of the United States. More than half (58%) of African Americans under age 65 live in the South (figure 8.3). African Americans also represent a larger share of the population in the South (21%) than their average in the United States (13%). Hispanics reside predominantly in the South (34%) and the West (41%). However, only in the West is the proportion of Hispanics (19%) greater than the average in the United States (9%) Thus, policies and practices of states in the South and West are important determinants of access for Hispanics and African Americans.

Figure 8.3
Geographic distribution of study population, 1987
Persons under age 65

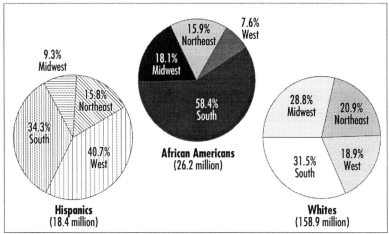

SOURCE: 1987 National Medical Expenditure Survey

Approximately 62.3 million white, Hispanic, and African Americans under age 65 are poor or near-poor (henceforth referred to as low-income). They consist of 10.2 million Hispanics, representing 56 percent of Hispanics; 14.7 million African Americans, or 56 percent of African Americans; and 37.4 million whites, or 24 percent of whites. A disproportionate share, about 40 percent, of low-income Americans under age 65, are Hispanic or African American (i.e. 10.2 million Hispanics and 14.7 million African Americans out of a total of 62.3 million low-income non-elderly persons).

To assess the extent to which governmental provisions have reduced inequities in access to care among nonelderly low-income Americans, several indicators of access are compared for whites, Hispanics, and African Americans residing in the Northeast, Midwest, South, and West. Racial/ethnic differences within the regions are assessed, and geographic differences across the regions are assessed for each racial/ethnic group. Differences in the ability to obtain care are examined using two measures: the percentage with Medicaid and the percent uninsured. Variation in the percentage without a routine physician visit in the past year (not including visits to the hospital emergency room) is examined as an indicator of realized access to care.

Overview

Racial/ethnic differences in health coverage among low-income Americans nationwide are displayed in figure 8.2. Low-income Americans obtain health coverage from private and public sources. Private coverage, however, plays a relatively minor role in the coverage of low-income Hispanics (26%) and African Americans (27%,) compared to whites (49%). Thus, Medicaid is an extremely important source of health coverage for minority populations. Given the relatively low rates of private coverage, the number of uninsured persons would likely be higher among African Americans were it not for Medicaid. Instead, low-income African Americans (32%) are no more likely to be uninsured than whites (33%). The Medicaid program, however, has not served a comparable role for Hispanics. Almost half (46%) of low-income Hispanics are uninsured and, therefore, at great disadvantage in obtaining care.

Although about 70 percent of African Americans and whites have either private coverage or Medicaid (figure 8.2), they differ in the care obtained. African Americans' use of physician services more closely resembles Hispanics' pattern of health service use than that of whites. While 36 percent of whites did not get routine care during the course of a year, about half of low-income Hispanics (47%) and African Americans (50%) did not get care (figure 8.4). Assuming a similar need for care among low-income Americans, these findings suggest racial/ethnic inequalities in access to care persist nationwide. They also show that a *sizable* share of low-income Americans of each racial/ethnic group did not get routine care during a year.

Medicaid Coverage by Region

An estimated 6.5 million low-income whites, 2.7 million low-income Hispanics, and 5.9 million low-income African Americans had health coverage through the Medicaid program in 1987 (table 8.4). Although Medicaid is perceived as a program that predominantly serves minority Americans, these data show that the program serves many whites as well. Medicaid is the major source of coverage for persons who are poor and has become an increasingly important source of coverage for the near-poor.

As discussed earlier, varying state Medicaid eligibility requirements result in variability in Medicaid coverage by geographic area. All things being equal, the more generous states would be expected to have more of their population covered by Medicaid and a smaller

Figure 8.4
Percent of poor/near-poor persons with no physician visit, 1987
Persons under age 65

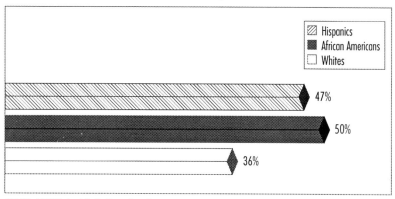

SOURCE: 1987 National Medical Expenditure Survey

share of the population uninsured. Unlike the uninsured, Medicaid beneficiaries have the financial means to pay for their care, even though they generally face problems in finding providers willing to accept Medicaid. Research, however, has shown that the poor with Medicaid use health services at rates comparable to the nonpoor (Newacheck 1988). Having publicly financed coverage, therefore, gives low-income Americans an advantage relative to the uninsured.

When comparing Medicaid coverage by region, geographic variations also are observed in the extent of coverage among Hispanics and African Americans (figure 8.5). Low-income African Americans in the Northeast are 1.5 times as likely to have Medicaid as their counterparts in the South (53% vs. 35%).[6] Similarly, low-income Hispanics in the Northeast are more than three times as likely to have Medicaid as their counterparts in the South (59% vs. 19%). Additionally, Hispanics in the Northeast are more likely to have Medicaid than their counterparts in the Midwest (34%) and West (25%). Medicaid coverage of Hispanics in the Northeast is clearly an anomaly. Higher rates of Medicaid coverage among Hispanics and African Americans in the Northeast are an indication that states in this region are more generous in their eligibility than are states in the other regions. Higher rates of coverage of Hispanics in the Northeast also may be an indication that more of the Hispanic population in this region are legal immigrants or U.S.-born, particularly since a substantial proportion of the Hispanics in the Northeast are Puerto Ricans, all of whom are U.S. citizens.

Racial/ethnic differences in Medicaid coverage are also apparent within several regions. African Americans have higher rates of Medicaid coverage than do whites of similar income in each region and, thus, may face advantages in obtaining coverage. However, the proportion of Hispanics and whites with Medicaid does not differ reliably except in the Northeast. In the Northeast, rates of Medicaid coverage are higher for Hispanics than for whites (59% vs. 19%).

The generally lower rates of Medicaid coverage among Hispanics and whites may be due to differences in family composition that affect eligibility. Since more African American families are headed by a single parent, categorical eligibility requirements that exclude two-parent families have a greater impact on Hispanic and white families than on African American families. Lower rates also may be a consequence of the undocumented immigration status of some low-income Hispanics. In addition, it is important to recall that low-income whites have private coverage at a rate almost twice that of low-income African Americans and Hispanics, leaving a smaller percentage of whites in need of Medicaid coverage.

Figure 8.5
Percent of poor/near-poor persons with Medicaid, by region, 1987
Persons under age 65

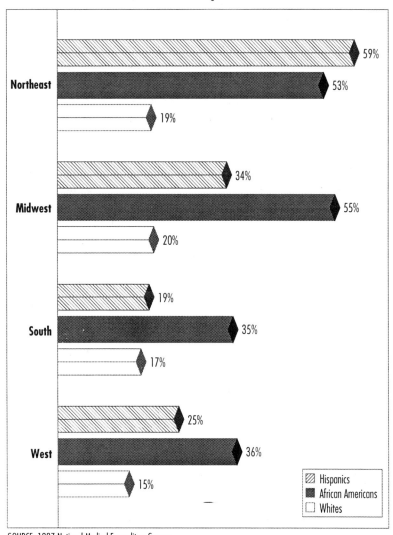

SOURCE: 1987 National Medical Expenditure Survey

Uninsured by Region

Misperceptions that the poor are all covered by Medicaid have led many to conclude that the uninsured are primarily middle-income Americans. Low-income Americans, however, are more likely to be uninsured than higher-income Americans. The number of low-income uninsured Americans is startling. An estimated 12.1 million low-income whites, 4.6 million low-income African Americans, and 4.5 million low-income Hispanics were uninsured in 1987 (table 8.5). The largest number (10.6 million) of low-income uninsured Americans live in the South.

Examining data on the uninsured across the regions provides evidence of geographic barriers to coverage in the South and in the West (figure 8.6). Low-income Hispanics in the South are nearly 3 times as likely to be uninsured as Hispanics in the Northeast (55% vs. 19%). Low-income African Americans in the South are 1.5 times as likely to be uninsured as their counterparts in the Northeast (37% vs. 25%). Similarly, low-income whites in the South are at least 1.5 times as likely to be uninsured as their counterparts in the Northeast or Midwest (39% vs. 25% vs. 28%). In the West, whites and Hispanics are more likely than their respective counterparts in the Northeast to be uninsured. These findings are an indication that in addition to factors such as income and race/ethnicity, geographic-specific policies and practices are also determinants of health coverage.

Racial/ethnic differences in the uninsured are observed in two regions. Consistent with nationwide estimates, low-income African Americans are no more likely to be uninsured than whites in each of the regions. Hispanics, however, appear to face greater barriers to coverage than whites or African Americans in the South and in the West. In the South, 1.4 times as many Hispanics as whites are uninsured (55% vs. 39%). In the West, about 1.3 times as many Hispanics as whites are uninsured (49% vs. 39%). These findings are disconcerting since these two geographic areas have the largest concentration of Hispanics.

Use of Physician Services by Region

About 4.8 million low-income Hispanics, 7.4 million low-income African Americans, and 13.6 million low-income whites report not seeing a physician within a year (table 8.6). The numbers and percentage of a population without a routine physician visit are revealing indicators of access to care. Since physicians are the primary point of entry for preventive, primary, and specialty care,

Figure 8.6
Percent of poor/near-poor persons with no health coverage, by region, 1987
Persons under age 65

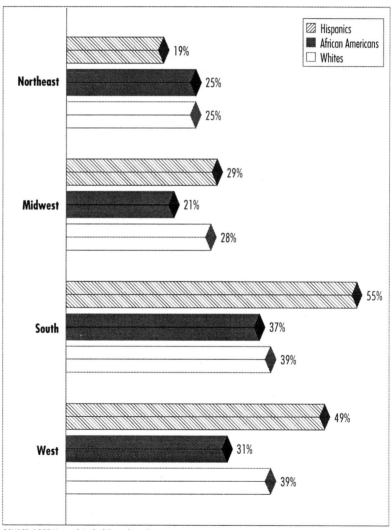

SOURCE: 1987 National Medical Expenditure Survey

the failure to visit a physician is a barometer for a population's access to a range of health services.

Examining the data across the regions reveals geographic differences in access to physician services (figure 8.7). Low-income African Americans in the South were more likely than their counterparts in the Midwest to not see a physician within a year (53% vs. 44%). Similarly, low-income whites in the South were more likely than their counterparts in the Midwest to not see a physician within a year (41% vs. 32%). Low-income Hispanics had equally poor access to physicians in all four regions, ranging from 46 percent of Hispanics not seeing a physician in the West to 49 percent in the South. These findings are an indication that geographic-specific factors contribute to and perhaps are primary determinants of the poorer access to care of African Americans and Whites in the South relative to their respective counterparts in the Midwest. For Hispanics, the findings suggest geographic-specific barriers to care, as well as barriers related to race/ethnicity.

Figure 8.7 also provides evidence of racial/ethnic differences in the use of physician services in all four regions. Disparities are largest in the Midwest and smallest in the South. Low-income Hispanics in the Midwest are 1.5 times as likely as low-income whites to not get routine care from a physician within a year (48% vs. 32%). Similarly, low-income African Americans in the Midwest are nearly 1.5 times as likely as low-income whites to not get routine care within a year (44% vs. 32%). Disparities, although smaller, also exist in the Northeast and West. Even in the South, which had the poorest access to care for all three racial groups, there was evidence that Hispanics and African Americans experience greater barriers to care than whites.[7]

DISCUSSION

Legal and ethical issues regarding equitable access to health care have been the subject of recurring debate in the United States. Much of the past health reform debate focused on defining how to balance public/private and federal/state responsibility in financing health-care costs. Less attention was devoted to analyzing the impact of various financing proposals on access to care. The debate on access has been less visible, in part, due to the acceptance by many Americans that health care is not a right, but a commodity to be purchased by those who can afford it.

Figure 8.7
Percent of poor/near-poor persons with no physician visit, by region, 1987
Persons under age 65

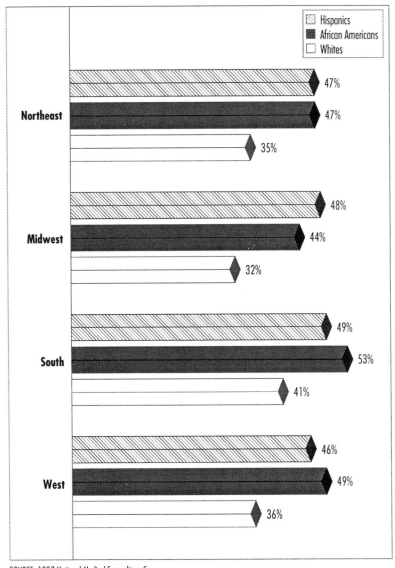

SOURCE: 1987 National Medical Expenditure Survey

An examination of the legal issues that undergird the debate about federal/state roles in health reveals that the Constitution gives legislators tremendous flexibility in establishing the limits or requirements for authority to be given to each governmental sector. As noted, both the federal and state governments have enacted provisions to improve access to care. Progress and setbacks have occurred as a result of actions and inactions in both sectors. The law and policy provisions that define the responsibilities of both sectors of government have substantive limitations that would likely impede their effectiveness in reducing current inequities in access. Some limitations are a function of the design of the provisions, some reflect problems in implementation, and others are a consequence of a health system that has evolved in a private sector with minimal public-sector oversight. Thus, responsibility for achieving standards of equitable access to care can build upon, but should not be limited by, existing law and policy.

The startlingly large share of low-income uninsured Americans under the current combination of federal and state programs suggests that without a system of universal health coverage some population groups will be at a disadvantage. Because minority populations are perceived as greater than average financial and health risks, there is little competition among providers or insurers for them. Regional variations in the uninsured are an indication that state-by-state health reform efforts would be an ineffective means of achieving universal coverage. Differences in coverage reflect variations in economic resources and in the industries that predominate in a geographic area. They also reflect state and regional differences in how constitutional rights are interpreted and in what is valued by the voting public. There is no evidence to suggest that these differences would not persist if states were given increased authority in the area of health.

Racial/ethnic disparities in access to physician services are also of concern. The disparities are small, but their consistency across regions suggests that they are not a consequence of policies and practices particular to a geographic area. The finding is an indication that racial/ethnic minority Americans with limited economic resources may be doubly at risk of facing barriers to care. At the very least, health reforms should eliminate payment distinctions that

186

reduce the buying power of publicly insured beneficiaries and permit providers to identify the economic status of the insured beneficiary. These distinctions inevitably place the beneficiary at risk for discrimination by health providers who seek to minimize their financial losses.

Increased state control in health-care financing and delivery could erode this nation's potential for achieving more equitable access to care nationwide. For example, payment reforms designed to improve access would likely be pursued by some but not all states resulting in lingering inequities across geographic areas. If state-based reforms are the primary focus of future health reforms, it will be important to create data collection systems at the state level with racial/ethnic identifiers. This information will be needed to monitor and evaluate the impact of state policies. When economic barriers combine with racial barriers, the risks are high, and the ability to distinguish between and document determinants of differentials is difficult. To facilitate the assessment of progress toward equitable access, uniform data collection and reporting systems will be needed.

Unquestionably, there are both benefits and shortcomings to strengthening the role of states in health. With stronger state involvement in health, there is the potential for gaining public input in the design and management of systems of care that may be better suited to local populations and conditions. However, many states with large populations of Hispanics and African Americans have higher poverty rates. Businesses may avoid states with more generous mandates for coverage because of the added financial burden of providing employer-based coverage. However, states with better coverage and benefits conceivably are at a disadvantage in a fairly mobile society of businesses and individuals. Some families could face undue burdens and would have fewer resources to meet this additional responsibility in efforts to relocate to states with coverage more favorable to their needs. Suppliers of health-care goods and services operate across state boundaries, as do businesses. The national character of the health industry and mobility of all players has potential consequences that are difficult to predict.

The persistence of racial/ethnic and geographic disparities and the weight of historical evidence argue strongly that this nation cannot afford to lessen the federal government's involvement in health.

Some states are either incapable (because of lack of financial resources) or unwilling to intervene to assure that economically disadvantaged minority populations do not face undue barriers in obtaining care. While some issues are more effectively handled at the state/local level by those most knowledgeable of the problem, others may necessitate a combined response from state and national lawmakers because of the national dimensions of the problem.

To assume that the federal government can now serve as the equalizer of past inequities given its current fiscal crisis and its poor relations with state governments may be unrealistic. The current approach of reducing financial barriers to care through the use of mandated expansions in coverage has produced a tension between federal and state officials that is counterproductive. The federal government is viewed as an intruder in the sovereign affairs of state and local governments. Nonetheless, it is important to acknowledge that the progress achieved to date is largely a consequence of federal initiatives that reduced financial barriers to care and enforced constitutional provisions that, in theory, guaranteed Hispanics and African Americans equality of opportunity but, in practice, were not enforced nationwide without federal legislative action. These efforts greatly helped to equalize access to care across geographic areas, income groups, and racial/ethnic groups.

A redefinition of the nature of the relationship between governmental partners is needed if this nation is to achieve further gains in access to care. The federal government has the authority and a proven track record in developing systems of financing of health care that work in concert with the private sector and are less costly to administer than private-sector insurance. States have knowledge and skill in developing local health-care resources that are responsive to the needs of their residents. Rather than deferring responsibility to the states, the federal government needs to share responsibility with the states to achieve nationally agreed-upon goals that seek to assure that health care, at a minimum, is financially accessible to a geographically, racially, and ethnically diverse U.S. population.

N*OTES*

1. The authors wish to thank Margaret H. Prendergast, Marguerite Ro, and Kristina Hanson for their work as research assistants and Phyllis Jones, Sara Rosenbaum, and Sally Schwartz for their thoughtful suggestions on an earlier version of this paper.

2. In 1824, John Marshall, Chief Justice of the United States Supreme Court, wrote that "health laws of every description" were included in "that immense mass of legislation, which embraces everything within the territory of a state, not surrendered to the general government, all of which can be most advantageously exercised by the states themselves." Gibbons v. Ogden, 22 U.S., Wheaton, 1, 89 (1824).

3. The Hill Burton Program, enacted in 1946, provided federal matching dollars for local governments to renovate, expand, or construct hospitals to equalize resources among the states and among urban and rural areas. Receipt of the funds was accompanied by a twenty-year obligation to provide a certain amount of uncompensated care for patients unable to pay. Current regulations specify that, in order to comply with its community service obligation, a facility receiving Hill-Burton funding under either the old or new program must make its services available to all persons residing, or in some cases employed, in the facility's service area, "without discrimination on the ground of race, color, national origin, creed, or any other ground unrelated to an individual's need for the service or the availability of the needed service."

4. The complaint alleges that it is impossible to determine the extent to which the poor health status and lesser access to health care suffered by African Americans are the result of racial discrimination because of DHHS's failure to collect and disseminate the data necessary for effective enforcement of Title VI. Further, without that data, effective enforcement of Title VI is impossible. Madison-Hughes v. Sullivan, (now Madison-Hughes v. Shalala), Civ. No. 393-0048 (M.D. Tenn. complaint filed Jan. 19, 1993).

5. ERISA states that its provisions "shall supersede any and all State laws insofar as they may now or hereafter relate to any employee benefit plan." 29 U.S.C. 1144(a). 29 U.S.C. 1001-1461. The "savings" clause of ERISA preserves states' rights to "regulate insurance." 29 U.S.C. 1144(b)(2)(A). However, an "employee benefit plan" is not an "insurance" company for purposes of any state law regulating insurance. 29 U.S.C. 1144(b)(2)(B). Therefore, any state law that attempts to regulate an employee benefit plan will be preempted by ERISA.

6. The share of African Americans with Medicaid in the West (36%) is not reliably different from the share in the Northeast and Midwest. The estimate could be unstable because of the relatively small number of African Americans who live in the West.

7. The percentage of African Americans without a physician visit differed reliably from the rate for whites in all four regions. Estimates of the use of physician services by Hispanics differed reliably from that of Whites only in the Midwest. The failure to find reliably different rates, however, could be a consequence of the smaller number of Hispanics when conducting analyses by region.

REFERENCES

Alcocer, P.D., D.J. Rasmussen, and R.A. Forland. 1994. *Health Insurance Regulation: Wide Variation in States' Authority, Oversight, and Resources.* GAO/HRD-94-26. Washington, DC: US General Accounting Office.

Altman, D.E., and D.H. Morgan. 1983. The role of state and local government in health. *Health Affairs* 2(4):7-31.

Arnold, J., A.E. Van Dusen, R.J. Baxter, and B. Carney. 1994. Undocumented persons in a health care reform environment. Lewin-VHI, Inc. Paper commissioned by the Kaiser Family Foundation.

Baumgartner, L., K.J. Campbell, P.K. Yamane, and S. Sternersen. 1994. *Health Professions Education: Role of Title VII/VIII Programs in Improving Access to Care Is Unclear.* GAO/HEHS-94-164. Washington, DC: US General Accounting Office.

Davis, K., M. Lillie-Blanton, B. Lyons, F. Mullan, N. Powe, and D. Rowland. 1989. Health care for black Americans: The public sector role. In *Health Policies and Black Americans,* edited by D. Willis. New Brunswick, NJ: Transaction Publishers.

Dowell, M. 1989. State and local government legal responsibilities to provide medical care for the poor. *Journal of Law and Health* 1(3):1988-1989.

Lewin, M.E., and B. Rice, eds. 1994. *Balancing the Scales of Opportunity.* Institute of Medicine. Washington, DC: National Academy Press.

Lillie-Blanton, M.D., S. Felt, P. Redmon, S. Renn, S. Machlin, and E. Wennar. 1992. Rural and urban hospital closures, 1985-1988: Operating and environmental characteristics that affect risk. *Inquiry* 29:332-344.

Link, C., S. Long, and R. Settle. 1982. Access to medical care under Medicaid: Differentials by race. *Journal of Health, Policy, and Law* 7(2):345-365.

Lipson, D.J. 1994. Keeping the promise? Achieving universal health coverage in six states. Alpha Center. Paper commissioned by the Kaiser Family Foundation.

Lockhart, W.B., Y. Kamisav, J.H. Chapps, and S.H. Shiffin. 1986. *Constitutional Law.* Minneapolis: West.

Loprest, P., and M. Gates. 1993. *State-Level Databook on Health Care Access and Financing*. Washington, DC: The Urban Institute.

National Association of State Budget Officers. 1994. *1993 State Expenditure Report*. Washington, DC.

Newacheck, P. 1988. Access to ambulatory services for poor persons. *Health Services Research* 23:401-409.

O'Brian, M., J. Rodgers, and D. Baugh. 1985. *Ethnic and Racial Patterns in Enrollment, Health Status, and Health Services Utilization in the Medicaid Population*. Series B, Descriptive Report No. 8. Washington, DC: US Department of Health and Human Services, Health Care Financing Administration.

Rowland, D., J. Feder, and A. Salganicoff, eds. 1993. *Medicaid Financing Crisis: Balancing Responsibilities, Priorities and Dollars*. Washington, DC: The Kaiser Commission on the Future of Medicaid.

Toiv, H.F., W.J. Schuyler, and M.A. Roskin. 1992. *Access to Health Care: States Respond to Growing Crisis*. GAO/HRD-92-70. Washington, DC: US General Accounting Office.

US Bureau of the Census. 1991. *Statistical Abstract of the United States: 1991*, Ed. II. Washington, DC.

US Commission on Civil Rights. 1980. *Civil Rights Issues in Health Care Delivery*. Washington, DC.

Table 8.1

Key federal laws affecting minority populations' ability to access care

PROVISION	DESCRIPTION
FINANCING TO EXPAND ACCESS TO COVERAGE AND TO SERVICES IN THE PRIVATE MARKETPLACE	
• Medicare A	• Federal health financing program for the elderly (age 65+) and disabled.
• Medicaid B	• Federal/state health financing program for certain categories of the poor.
• Disproportionate Share Hospital (DSH) payment provision of Medicaid C	• Additional payment to providers by HHS for provision of services where hospitals serve a disproportionate share of low-income people.
FINANCING TO DEVELOP HEALTH RESOURCES (PROVIDERS AND FACILITIES)	
• Migrant and Community Health Centers (MHCs and CHCs) D	• MHCs provide a comprehensive range of primary health services to migrant and seasonal farmworkers and their dependents. CHCs provide basic primary medical services to persons located in rural and urban areas with financial, geographic, or cultural barriers to care.
• Public Health Service Act; Title VII: Physicians, dentists, physician assistants, and allied health professionals E; Title VIII: Nurses, nurse practitioners, and nurse-midwives F	• Since 1962, Congress has established over 40 programs to improve the supply and distribution of health providers. Of these, at least eight programs targeted the recruitment and retention of health professionals from minority and/or disadvantaged backgrounds.
• The Disadvantaged Minority Health Improvement Act, 1990 G	• Established the Office of Minority Health within the Office of the Assistant Secretary of Health. Provides grant programs and medical and health education loan programs for improvement of minority health.

Continued on next page

193

Table 8.1 continued

PROVISION	DESCRIPTION
PROTECTIONS TO REDUCE THE POTENTIAL FOR DISCRIMINATION BY PROVIDERS ON THE BASIS OF RACE, INCOME, PUBLIC INSURANCE STATUS, OR DISABILITY	
• The Hill-Burton Act H	• Provided federal matching dollars for local governments to renovate, expand, or construct hospitals in order to equalize resources among states and among urban/rural areas. The recipients of such funds made certain assurances known as the "community service obligation and the uncompensated care obligation."
• Title VI of the Civil Rights Act, 1964 I	• Prohibits discrimination by a service provider that receives federal funds. Provides for enforcement in the event of a breach of the statute or regulations.
• The Emergency Medical Treatment and Active Labor Act J	• Enacted to combat the practice by hospitals of refusing to treat patients unable to pay or transferring such patients to another, usually public, hospital. Hospitals under Medicare agreements cannot transfer or discharge a patient who has an "emergency medical condition" or who is in active labor.
• Section 504 of the Rehabilitation Act of 1973 K	• Prohibits discrimination against people with disabilities by recipients of federal funds, the federal government itself, and federal contractors.
• The Americans with Disabilities Act, 1990 L	• Prohibits discrimination on the basis of disability by private entities in the workplace and places of public accommodation. Requires new places of public accommodation and commercial facilities to be designed and constructed to be readily accessible by persons with disabilities. Combines elements of the Civil Rights Act of 1964 and Title V of the Rehabilitation Act of 1973.

A 42 USC sect. 1396 (a)
B 42 USC sect. 1396
C Consolidated Omnibus Budget Reconciliation Act (COBRA) of 1985
D Sections 329 and 330 of the PHS Act
E 1963
F 1964
G 42 USC sect. 3004 et seq.

H The Hospital Survey and Construction Act of 1946, P.L., 42 USC sect. 291 et seq.; superseded by the National Health Planning and Resources Act of 1975, P.L.
I 42 USC sect. 601-2/ 42 USC 2000d
J 42 USC sect. 1395dd
K 29 USC sect. 794
L 42 USC sect. 12102(2)

194

Table 8.2

Key state-administered laws and programs affecting minority populations' ability to access care

PROVISION A	DESCRIPTION
FINANCING TO EXPAND ACCESS TO COVERAGE AND TO SERVICES IN THE PRIVATE MARKETPLACE	
• Medicaid B	• Federal/state health financing program for certain categories of the poor.
• Provider payment mechanisms, trust funds	• Hospital rate-setting mechanisms, trust funds.
PROVISION OF SERVICES DIRECTLY	
• Preventive health services	• Traditional public health functions of infectious disease control, immunization.
• Primary care services	• Community clinics, neighborhood health services for the medically indigent.
• Public hospitals	• Provide inpatient, primary, and specialty care services.
REGULATION OF INSURANCE INDUSTRY BY STATE INSURANCE DEPARTMENT	
• License and monitor insurer financial solvency	• State legislatures establish rules under which insurance companies must operate, enforced by state insurance departments. They approve rates and protect consumers from unfair business practices.
• McCarren-Ferguson Act of 1945	• Affirmed the primary responsibility of states for regulating the insurance industry.
• National Association of Insurance Commissioners (NAIC)	• A voluntary association consisting of heads of the insurance departments of the 50 states, the District of Columbia, and four US Territories. The NAIC model laws, regulations, and guidelines models are not mandatory, but some states have adopted the same or similar models.

Continued on next page

195

Table 8.2 continued

PROVISION	DESCRIPTION
• Employee Retirement Income Security Act (ERISA)	• Constrains the ability of states to regulate employer-sponsored health funds that choose to self-insure. The ERISA exemption, as interpreted by the Supreme Court, has produced a divided system for regulating health benefits in each state such that the federal government has authority to regulate self-insured employee health plans, but not health policies sold by insurance companies.
CONSTITUTIONAL REQUIREMENT	
• Fourteenth Amendment to the US Constitution	• Equal protection clause prohibits discrimination based on race, national origin, or alienage.

A Legislative provisions, if any, vary by state. Health care policies and statutes are developed under a state's B 42 USC sect. 1396.
broad police powers to regulate for the health, safety, and welfare of its citizens. 42 USC sect. 1396 (a).

Table 8.3
Medicaid profile for persons under age 65 by region and race/ethnicity

	HISPANIC AND AFRICAN AMERICAN POPULATION, 1987		MEDICAID CHARACTERISTICS, 1990		
	African American[A] (percent)	Hispanic[A] (percent)	Poor with Medicaid[B] (percent)	Ratio of Medicaid fees to private fees[C]	Average expenditure per enrollee[D] (dollars)
UNITED STATES	12.9	9.0	49	0.59	1,291
NORTHEAST					
New England	4.6	3.7	57	0.62	1,328
Middle Atlantic	11.7	7.8	58	0.35	1,756
MIDWEST					
East N. Central	9.9	4.1	57	0.60	1,128
West N. Central	6.6	0.9	46	0.66	1,166
SOUTH					
South Atlantic	23.7	3.7	45	0.66	1,408
East S. Central	23.3	0.5	45	0.69	1,384
West S. Central	15.7	23.2	38	0.84	1,368
WEST					
Mountain	3.6	14.8	37	0.67	1,237
Pacific	5.8	19.8	54	0.51	1,051

SOURCE: 1987 National Medical Expenditure Survey

[A] These are weighted population percents, derived from the NMES sample, to be representative of the U.S. population. In 1987, there were an estimated 18.4 million Hispanics and 26.2 million African Americans in the U.S. population.

[B] Persons under age 65 with incomes below 100 percent of poverty (Loprest and Gates 1993, Table A12)

[C] All services (Loprest and Gates 1993, Table D10)

[D] Adults ages 18-65 (Loprest and Gates 1993, Table D5).

Table 8.4
Poor/near poor with Medicaid, 1987
Persons under age 65

REGION	TOTAL	WHITES	AFRICAN AMERICANS	HISPANICS
NUMBERS IN MILLIONS				
Total	15.1	6.5	5.9	2.7
Northeast	3.0	1.2	1.0	0.8
Midwest	3.9	2.1	1.4	0.3
South	6.1	2.2	3.2	0.7
West	2.1	0.9	0.9	0.9
PERCENT OF THE POPULATION (95% CI) A				
Total	24.8	17.7 (15.3–20.0)	40.7 (37.0–44.4)	28.0 (23.9–32.1)
Northeast	30.8	18.6 (13.3–24.0)	53.1 (45.1–61.2)	59.2 (51.1–67.6)
Midwest	27.1	20.0 (15.7–24.4)	55.4 (48.3–62.5)	33.8 (17.1–50.4)
South	23.3	16.5 (12.1–21.1)	34.7 (30.1–39.2)	18.9 (14.7–23.1)
West	19.9	15.0 (9.7–20.3)	36.0 (19.2–52.9)	24.8 (17.6–32.0)

SOURCE: 1987 National Medical Expenditure Survey
A CI indicates confidence interval.

Table 8.5
Poor/near-poor with no health coverage, 1987
Persons under age 65

REGION	TOTAL	WHITES	AFRICAN AMERICANS	HISPANICS
NUMBERS IN MILLIONS				
Total	21.2	12.1	4.6	4.5
Northeast	2.4	1.6	0.6	0.3
Midwest	3.9	3.0	0.5	0.3
South	10.6	5.0	3.4	2.1
West	4.5	2.4	0.2	1.8
PERCENT OF THE POPULATION (95% CI) A				
Total	34.9 (32.9–36.9)	33.1 (30.7–35.6)	31.9 (29.1–34.7)	45.6 (40.7–50.5)
Northeast	24.3 (20.4–28.3)	25.3 (21.3–29.4)	24.5 (16.1–32.9)	19.3 (9.5–29.2)
Midwest	26.9 (22.9–31.0)	28.2 (23.4–33.0)	20.8 (15.9–25.7)	28.8 (12.2–45.4)
South	40.3 (37.0–43.5)	38.6 (34.2–43.0)	36.5 (33.3–39.7)	55.1 (48.4–61.8)
West	41.7 (38.1–45.3)	38.5 (34.3–42.7)	30.5 (21.4–39.6)	49.4 (43.4–55.4)

SOURCE: 1987 National Medical Expenditure Survey
A CI indicates confidence interval.

Table 8.6
Poor/near-poor with no physician visits, 1987
Persons under age 65

REGION	TOTAL	WHITES	AFRICAN AMERICANS	HISPANICS
NUMBERS IN MILLIONS				
Total	25.8	13.6	7.4	4.8
Northeast	3.8	2.3	1.9	0.6
Midwest	5.1	3.5	1.1	0.5
South	12.5	5.5	5.0	2.0
West	4.5	2.3	0.4	1.8
PERCENT OF THE POPULATION (95% CI) A				
Total	41.5 (39.8–43.2)	36.4 (34.3–38.6)	50.4 (47.3–53.5)	47.3 (42.8–51.8)
Northeast	39.0 (36.1–42.0)	35.1 (31.2–39.0)	47.4 (42.3–52.5)	46.8 (37.4–56.2)
Midwest	34.8 (31.3–38.3)	31.6 (28.4–34.8)	43.5 (37.8–49.1)	48.0 (40.9–55.1)
South	46.4 (43.6–49.3)	41.1 (36.5–45.6)	53.0 (48.6–57.4)	48.8 (40.4–57.2)
West	40.6 (36.5–44.7)	36.4 (33.1–39.7)	49.4 (41.1–57.6)	45.7 (38.1–53.3)

SOURCE: 1987 National Medical Expenditure Survey
A CI indicates confidence interval.

Summary of Findings and Policy Implications

The U.S. health care system is unquestionably at a crossroads. Even though the United States has achieved tremendous gains in making access to care more equitable in the last 25 years, the nation's system for financing and delivering health services continues to exclude millions of Americans and inadequately care for others. This is a reality even though per capita spending within the U.S. health system is greater than in the health systems of most other industrialized nations. Race and ethnicity in the United States continue to be powerful determinants of life experiences and opportunities. Although low-income minority groups experience the most acute barriers in access to care, higher-income Hispanics and African Americans also confront barriers.

Because of these continuing disparities, it is vital that issues that especially affect racial/ethnic minority groups be considered as policymakers continue to debate how to reform our health-care system. Many of the issues that have been brought to the forefront in the deliberations about health-care reform are of concern to most Americans regardless of income or race/ethnicity—for example, portability of coverage, coverage for preexisting conditions, and choice in selecting health providers. However, other issues, specific to the historic conditions and current circumstances of Hispanics and African Americans, also deserve consideration in the policy debate. The research project that yielded this book was undertaken to provide policymakers, practitioners, and advocates with an objective account of the progress achieved in enhancing access to care and the nature of problems that persist for these groups.

If further gains in reducing racial/ethnic disparities are to be achieved, a combination of strategies will be required, including some restructuring of the financing and service delivery systems that have been built over the last 30 years. The existing mix of public/private financing is flawed in many respects, but it also has made possible the gains achieved to date. The public/private service delivery infrastructure within Hispanic and African American communities is generally undercapitalized and ill-equipped for the transitions currently occurring in these systems. Nonetheless, until a better system can be created, the challenge facing those concerned with the health of minority populations is to build upon the existing foundation and to resist political pressures and program initiatives threatening to erode the systems of care now serving millions of uninsured and underinsured minority Americans.

Through the analysis of national survey data and discussions at policy forums organized by the project, several issues have emerged as key for remedying the inequities described in this book.

SYSTEM OF UNIVERSAL COVERAGE

Of utmost importance is the need for a system of health insurance coverage in this country that is not determined by differences in income or employment. Without greater equality in the opportunity to obtain coverage, the current disparities will persist. Inequities in health insurance coverage have consequences for the availability of health resources in low-income communities and compromise the health of a sizable sector of the population.

Given an increasingly diverse workforce, reducing inequities in access to coverage is a social investment. Including all Americans in the system of health insurance coverage not only is an issue of fairness but also could foster the development of a health-care sector that is financially sound. It is shortsighted and ultimately costly public policy to exclude millions of Americans—who in percentages are disproportionately Hispanics and African Americans, though in absolute numbers are primarily whites—from the benefits of the U.S. health-care system.

SOCIOCULTURAL COMPETENCE OF THE HEALTH SYSTEM

This research provides evidence of the importance of systems of care that are socioculturally competent. Obstacles to care sometimes arise from responses to sociocultural differences, which can reflect the prejudices of providers or patients either about racial/ethnic minority groups or about institutional practices. In other cases, obstacles to care arise from insufficient and inaccurate information or differences in expectations. Access to care, therefore, is hindered by individual attitudes, such as patients' distrust of providers and the prejudices of providers themselves. Moreover, these patient and provider attitudes heavily influence each other, with new barriers arising from negative experiences.

Some of the cultural insensitivities of providers are not intentional efforts to discourage the use of health resources, but arise from a lack of awareness about social customs or about the social environment of the populations served. For example, providers may be unaware that services usually defined as ancillary (e.g., transportation, translation, and interpreters) are in fact essential for access by some low-income minority patients. One means of promoting cultural and linguistic competency is to increase support for the training, recruitment, and retention of a workforce that reflects the sociocultural composition of the communities served. In short, public and private health providers must become more sensitive and responsive to these and other needs of a diverse client population.

THE IMPORTANCE OF A REGULAR PROVIDER

The analyses in this volume provide evidence that health insurance coverage is necessary but not sufficient for improving access to care. Among both insured and uninsured alike, having a regular provider also was an important determinant of access. Moreover, having any regular provider was a more important determinant of access than the type of caregiver (i.e., a private physician, a community health center, or hospital-based primary-care site). Thus, efforts to improve the health services delivery infrastructure within and available to minority communities are important. Assuring that every individual has a regular provider, one that is both geographically accessible and culturally competent, should be the goal.

PUBLIC/PRIVATE ROLES IN ASSURING EQUITABLE ACCESS

Finally, the persistence of geographic and racial/ethnic disparities weakens the capacity of the nation as a whole to face the challenges ahead. Yet, the current public-private mix of health coverage reflects state- and region-specific differences in employment and financial resources. Remedying these inequities cannot be the sole responsibility of either the federal or the state governments. With the reduction of federal funds for local services beginning in the 1980s, many state and local governments now have inadequate resources to manage current services, much less to expand services to meet new areas of need. As such, a shared responsibility is required, with a combination of approaches at all levels of government.

The current political climate discourages the use of government planning and regulatory mechanisms to achieve the national goal of equitable access. Many argue that market forces can and should correct deficiencies in the U.S. health system. Yet historically, government has intervened in the market for health-care services because of the inability or, in some cases, unwillingness of the private sector to address long-standing problems in access. If current practices and policies are maintained, there is little basis to assume that market forces will respond any differently now than in the past to those who are uninsured or inadequately insured.

Although the sentiment of the voting public toward the role of government certainly has shifted, there is little evidence that the public wants government to abandon entirely its responsibilities in the area of health care. There is considerable evidence, however, that the public wants government to perform its job in the most efficient and cost-effective manner possible. As such, there is an urgent need to heighten awareness and achieve some level of consensus on public/private and federal/state roles in assuring equitable access to care.

The National Medical Expenditure Survey: A Description of the Database

DATA SOURCE

To provide policymakers, practitioners, and advocates with an objective account of the nation's progress in reducing barriers to care that confront Hispanics and African Americans, the studies published in this volume analyzed the 1987 National Medical Expenditure Survey (NMES) data. NMES, sponsored by the U.S. Department of Health and Human Services, provides the most nationally representative estimates of health care use and expenditures that are currently available. The research undertaken for this volume represents the most comprehensive examination of the NMES data with a focus on Hispanics and African Americans.

METHODOLOGY

NMES obtained information from a nationally representative sample of the civilian noninstitutionalized population in the continental United States. The survey was fielded in four interview rounds at approximately four month intervals. The study design included an oversampling of low-income, African American, and Hispanic households. The household sample, selected using a stratified multistage probability design, consisted of 36,400 individuals in roughly 15,000 households.[1] Data were obtained for about 86 percent of eligible households in the first round of interviews and 80 percent in the fourth round.

---

[1] For a detailed description of the questionnaire design and data collection procedures, see W.S. Edwards and M. Berlin, *Questionnaires and Data Collection Methods for the Household Survey and the Survey of American Indians and Alaska Natives.* National Medical Expenditure Survey: Method, No. 2. DHHS pub. no. (PHS) 89-3450. (Rockville, MD: US Department of Health and Human Services, Public Health Service, 1989).

Project researchers primarily analyzed data collected during the first round of interviews. The statistical package SUDAAN (Professional Software for SUrvey DAta ANalysis)[2] was used to obtain weighted population estimates and standard errors. This package allows weights to correct for oversampling and biases due to nonresponse and the complex multistage sampling design of NMES. All but one research team used SUDAAN in developing estimates and testing relationships between measures of health services use or expenditures.[3]

---

[2] Research Triangle Institute, Research Triangle Park, NC

[3] The research team of Thornton and White-Means chose not to use SUDAAN. These authors acknowledge that SUDAAN could yield slightly larger standard errors, resulting in some statistically significant variables becoming insignificant. The authors, however, note that population characteristics used in the sampling design were controlled in the multivariate analysis to account for possible sources of bias due to oversampling. Thus, they have confidence in their results.

About the Authors and Project Staff

EDITORS

Marsha D. Lillie-Blanton, Dr.P.H.

Dr. Lillie-Blanton, director of the Johns Hopkins component of this project and coauthor of its summary report, *In the Nation's Interest: Equity in Access to Health Care*, is an assistant professor in the Department of Health Policy and Management at the Johns Hopkins University School of Public Health. She also is currently an associate director of the Kaiser Commission on the Future of Medicaid. Dr. Lillie-Blanton earned her Dr.P.H. from the Johns Hopkins University School of Public Health.

Wilhelmina A. Leigh, Ph.D.

Dr. Leigh, manager of the component of the project completed by the Joint Center for Political and Economic Studies, is a senior research associate at the Center. Her research interests include women's health, substance abuse treatment, HIV/AIDS prevention education, and health-care reform. Dr. Leigh earned her Ph.D. in economics from the School of Arts and Sciences at Johns Hopkins University.

Ana I. Alfaro-Correa, Sc.D.

Dr. Alfaro-Correa, coauthor of the project summary report, is currently a research fellow in the Department of Epidemiology and Preventive Medicine at the University of Maryland School of Medicine. She earned her Sc.D. from the Johns Hopkins University School of Public Health.

AUTHORS

Jared Bernstein, Ph.D.

Dr. Bernstein, a labor economist at the Economic Policy Institute, does research on labor markets, wage and employment trends, income and earnings inequality, and issues related to poverty. He earned his Ph.D. in social welfare from Columbia University.

Felipe G. Castro, Ph.D.

Dr. Castro is an associate professor in the Department of Psychology and has served as director of the Hispanic Research Center at the Arizona State University. His research interests include the prevention and treatment of AIDS and drug and alcohol abuse. Dr. Castro earned his Ph.D. in clinical psychology at the University of Washington.

Kathryn Coe, Ph.D.

Dr. Coe serves as a research administrator for Companeros en la Salud with the Hispanic Research Center at the Arizona State University. Her research interest is in the effect of cultural change on health and fertility. Dr. Coe holds a Ph.D. in anthropology from Arizona State University, where she also earned her master's degree in anthropology.

Llewellyn J. Cornelius, Ph.D.

Dr. Cornelius is assistant professor in the School of Social Work at the University of Maryland at Baltimore, where he conducts research on access to medical care for minority populations and the underserved. Dr. Cornelius earned his Ph.D. in social services administration from the University of Chicago.

Mary Harmon, M.A.

Ms. Harmon was a senior research specialist at the Hispanic Research Center at the Arizona State University between 1992 and 1994. She currently works for the AIDS Research Consortium in Atlanta, Georgia. Her research interests are in sociology and demography. Her M.A. in sociology is from the University of Kentucky, and she also has taken Ph.D. courses in rural sociology and demography at the Pennsylvania State University.

Verna M. Keith, Ph.D.

Dr. Keith is an associate professor in the Department of Sociology at the Arizona State University. She earned her Ph.D. in sociology from the University of Kentucky and has research interests in mental health and health care utilization.

Thomas A. LaVeist, Ph.D.

Dr. LaVeist is an assistant professor in the Department of Health Policy and Management at the Johns Hopkins University School of Public Health. His research interests are in social and behavioral factors that influence and explain racial differences in health outcomes. Dr. LaVeist holds a Ph.D. in sociology from the University of Michigan.

Charisse Lillie, J.D., LL.M.

Ms. Lillie is a partner in the Philadelphia law firm of Ballard, Spahr, Andrews & Ingersoll. She is the former city solicitor of the City of Philadelphia and a former trial attorney in the U.S. Justice Department, Civil Rights Division. She earned a J.D. from Temple Law School and an LL.M. from Yale Law School.

M. Edith Rasell, M.D.

Dr. Rasell, a former family practitioner, is an economist at the Economic Policy Institute in Washington, D.C., where she conducts economic research in health care financing and labor market issues. Dr. Rasell is a graduate of the St. Louis University School of Medicine and has studied health economics at American University.

Linda C. Perkowski, M.S.

Ms. Perkowski is a Ph.D. candidate in preventive medicine and community health (with a concentration in sociomedical sciences) at the University of

Texas Medical Branch. In addition, she is a faculty associate in the Department of Internal Medicine and assistant editor for the *Journal of Aging and Health*. Ms. Perkowski holds an M.S. with a concentration in clinical psychology from Texas A&M University.

Christine A. Stroup-Benham, Ph.D.

Dr. Stroup-Benham is an assistant professor in the Department of Family Medicine and a senior associate in the Office of Educational Development (OED) at the University of Texas Medical Branch. Her research interests include preventive cardiology and Hispanic health issues. Dr. Stroup-Benham earned her Ph.D. in the Department of Preventive Medicine at the University of Texas Medical Branch.

Zulema E. Suarez, Ph.D.

Dr. Suarez is an assistant professor in the School of Social Work at the University of Michigan. Her research interest is in self health care and formal health care utilization by Hispanic subgroups and women. Dr. Suarez earned her Ph.D., with an emphasis on policy and clinical programs, at the School of Social Services of the University of Chicago.

Michael C. Thornton, Ph.D.

Dr. Thornton is an assistant professor at the University of Wisconsin at Madison, where he also directs the Asian Studies Program. His research interests are families and ethnicity. Dr. Thornton holds a Ph.D. in sociology from the University of Michigan.

Shelley I. White-Means, Ph.D.

Dr. White-Means is a professor of economics at the University of Memphis and a member of the National Academy of Social Insurance, based in Washington, D.C. Her research area is health services utilization patterns of racial and ethnic minority groups. Dr. White-Means has a Ph.D. in economics from Northwestern University.

Ruth E. Zambrana, Ph.D.

Professor Zambrana holds the Enoch chair and is the director of the Child Welfare Center at George Mason University. She was previously a senior research scientist at the Agency for Health Care Policy and Research. Her research interests are maternal, child, and adolescent health in low-income, racial, and ethnic groups. Dr. Zambrana earned her Ph.D. in sociology at Boston University.

PROJECT STAFF

Leslie Allen

Ms. Allen served as administrative assistant for the project. She is currently working toward a B.S. degree in health sciences at the University of Maryland.

Howard D. Chilcoat, Sc.D., M.S., M.H.S.

Dr. Chilcoat, the project's statistician, is a research scientist in the Department of Psychiatry at Henry Ford Health Sciences Center in Detroit, Michigan. He was previously a staff fellow in the Division of Intramural Research of the National Institute of Drug Abuse. Dr. Chilcoat earned his Sc.D. from the Johns Hopkins University School of Public Health.

Darrell J. Gaskin, M.S., Ph.D.

Dr. Gaskin, the project's data manager and supervising computer programmer, was a doctoral student while the project was underway. He is currently an instructor/research associate at the Georgetown University Medical School's Institute for Health Care Research and Policy. Dr. Gaskin earned his M.S. in economics at MIT and his Ph.D. in health economics from the Johns Hopkins University School of Public Health.

Mary Lou Gutierrez-Mohamed, Sc.D.

Dr. Gutierrez-Mohamed, one of the project's computer programmers, was a doctoral student while the project was underway. She is currently a research fellow with the National Cancer Institute. Dr. Gutierrez-Mohamed earned her Sc.D., with a concentration in health services research, from the Johns Hopkins University School of Public Health.

José R. Muñoz, Ph.D.

Dr. Muñoz, the project's associate director, has research interests in minority health, access to care, and sociocultural barriers to health care. Prior to joining the project at Johns Hopkins, Dr. Muñoz served as public affairs officer for the National Coalition of Hispanic Health and Human Services Organizations (COSSMHO). He received both the M.Ed. and Ph.D. degrees from Pennsylvania State University and is currently an assistant professor in the Department of Foreign Languages at St. Mary's College.

Ruth Rios, M.S.

Ms. Rios, one of the project's computer programmers, is a doctor of science candidate in the School of Public Health at Johns Hopkins University. Her research interest is in minority health and evaluation. Ms. Rios earned her M.S. with a major in health research and evaluation at the University of Puerto Rico.

List of Reviewers and Project Roundtable Participants

REVIEWERS

The following people offered their expertise in reviewing the research published in this volume.

Professor Antonio Furino, Ph.D.
Director, Center for Health Economics and Policy
University of Texas Health Sciences Center
San Antonio, TX

Professor Alvin Headen, Ph.D.
Department of Economics and Business, North Carolina State University
Raleigh, NC

LaRah Payne, Sc.D.
Howard University Hospital
Washington, DC

Rueben Warren, D.D.S., M.P.H.
Assistant Director for Minority Health
Centers for Disease Control and Prevention
Atlanta, GA

PROJECT ROUNDTABLE PARTICIPANTS

The following people participated in a research and policy roundtable sponsored by the Joint Center for Political and Economic Studies on April 20, 1993. The event provided a forum for discussing many of the ideas investigated in the papers in this volume.

Irma Arispe, Ph.D.
Agency for Health Care Policy and Research
U.S. Department of Health and Human Services
Rockville, MD

Thomas Chapman, M.P.H., F.A.C.H.E.
George Washington University and George Washington University Hospital
Washington, DC

Llewellyn J. Cornelius, Ph.D.
University of Maryland at Baltimore, School of Social Work
Baltimore, MD

211

Pat Golden, M.S.
National Center for Health Statistics
Centers for Disease Control and Prevention
Hyattsville, MD

Miriam Kelly, Ph.D.
MEDTEP Program, Agency for Health Care Policy and Research
U.S. Department of Health and Human Services
Rockville, MD

Sally Kohn, M.P.H.
Opening Doors Program
Washington, DC

Rose Martinez, Sc.D.
Mathematica Policy Research
Washington, DC

LaRah Payne, Sc.D.
Howard University Hospital
Washington, DC

Shelley I. White-Means, Ph.D.
University of Memphis
Memphis, TN

Ruth E. Zambrana, Ph.D.
George Mason University
Fairfax, VA

JOINT CENTER FOR POLITICAL AND ECONOMIC STUDIES

ACHIEVING EQUITABLE ACCESS

Edited by Marsha Lillie-Blanton, Wilhelmina Leigh, and Ana Alfaro-Correa

Manuscript Editing: Mary Garber

Proofreading: Marc DeFrancis, Jerry Richards (EEI Inc.)

Word Processing: Bettina Lucas

Text and Cover Design: Theresa Kilcourse

JOINT CENTER BOOKS OF RELATED INTEREST

Economic Perspectives on Affirmative Action
Margaret Simms, editor

The Declining Economic Status of Black Children:
Examining the Change
Cynthia Rexroat

African Americans Today: A Demographic Profile
Compiled by Doris Warriner

Young Black Males in Jeopardy: Risk Factors and Intervention Strategies
Alex Poinsett and Margaret Simms

For ordering information, call the Joint Center at 202-789-3500.